Communications
in Computer and Information Science   597

Commenced Publication in 2007
Founding and Former Series Editors:
Alfredo Cuzzocrea, Dominik Ślęzak, and Xiaokang Yang

Anabel Martin-Gonzalez · Victor Uc-Cetina (Eds.)

Intelligent Computing Systems

First International Symposium, ISICS 2016
Mérida, México, March 16–18, 2016
Proceedings

 Springer

Editors
Anabel Martin-Gonzalez
Universidad Autónoma de Yucatán
Mérida, Yucatán
México

Victor Uc-Cetina
Universidad Autónoma de Yucatán
Mérida, Yucatán
México

ISSN 1865-0929 ISSN 1865-0937 (electronic)
Communications in Computer and Information Science
ISBN 978-3-319-30446-5 ISBN 978-3-319-30447-2 (eBook)
DOI 10.1007/978-3-319-30447-2

Library of Congress Control Number: 2015959587

Printed on acid-free paper

This Springer imprint is published by SpringerNature
The registered company is Springer International Publishing AG Switzerland

Preface

Intelligent systems are computer systems capable of perceiving, reasoning, learning, and acting rationally, always maximizing an evaluation function. Several kinds of algorithmic methods could be used in the implementation of this type of system, methods such as neural networks, Bayesian networks, kernel machines, feature extraction and dimension reduction, deep learning, reinforcement learning, self-organizing maps, optimization methods in learning, fuzzy systems, and evolutionary computation, among others.

With the increase in the number of personal computers, smart phones, and computer servers, the need for the development of intelligent systems has also experienced an important increment. Moreover, the current speed of computer processors allows for the implementation of algorithms that run on bigger databases. Many of these applications are implemented as Web services that can be accessed via smart phones and tablets.

Now more than ever the development of intelligent systems is playing a main role in fields such as biology, computer vision, robotics, search engines, and big data, to name a few. An increasing number of new algorithms and applications are proposed and developed each year.

This book contains the written contributions of the First International Symposium on Intelligent Computing Systems (ISICS) that was held in Mérida (México), during March 16–18, 2016. To further increase the body of knowledge in this specific area of computer science was the aim of ISICS 2016, by providing a forum for attendees to exchange ideas and discuss state-of-the-art results. The ISICS 2016 was committed to the promotion, preservation, and collaboration of research and practice, focusing on the fields of artificial intelligence, computer vision, and image processing.

We received 22 submissions from 15 different countries around the world. Each submission was evaluated by at least three members of the Program Committee and external reviewers. Based on these reviews, 12 papers were selected for long oral presentation. In addition to the contributed papers, four keynote speaker presentations were included in the conference program.

We want to thank the authors for their contributions, the scientific Program Committee members for their reviews and especially our invited speakers, Prof. Raúl Rojas (FU-Berlin), Prof. Carlos Coello Coello (CINVESTAV), Prof. Ángel Kuri Morales (ITAM), and Prof. Petar Kormushev (ICL). We are very grateful to the Universidad Nacional Autónoma de México (UNAM), the Centro de Investigaciones Matemáticas (CIMAT), and the Universidad Autónoma de Yucatán (UADY) for their support in the organization of ISICS 2016. Finally, we wish to thank Prof. Carlos Brito-Loeza (UADY) and Prof. Arturo Espinosa-Romero (UADY) for their invaluable help in coordinating the double-blind peer-review process.

March 2016

Anabel Martin-Gonzalez
Victor Uc-Cetina

Organization

Scientific Advisory Committee

Carlos A. Coello Coello	CINVESTAV, México
Ángel Kuri Morales	Instituto Tecnológico Autónomo de México, México
Juan Arturo Nolazco Flores	ITESM-Monterrey, México
Raúl Rojas	Freie Universität Berlin, Germany
Adolfo Sánchez Valenzuela	Centro de Investigaciones en Matemáticas, México

Program Committee

Jorge Armando Argáez Sosa	Universidad Autónoma de Yucatán
Muhammad Asad	City University London, UK
Noor Badshah	University of Engineering and Technology, Pakistan
Ali Bassam	Universidad Autónoma de Yucatán, México
Carlos Brito-Loeza	Universidad Autónoma de Yucatán, México
Héctor Gibrán Ceballos Cancino	ITESM, México
Morgado Dias	Universidade da Madeira, Portugal
Arturo Espinosa-Romero (Chair)	Universidad Autónoma de Yucatán, México
Carlos Gershenson García	IIMAS-UNAM, México
Jorge Gómez-Montalvo	Universidad Autónoma de Yucatán, México
Benjamin Gutierrez Becker	Technische Universität München, Germany
Joaquín Gutiérrez Jaguey	Centro de Investigaciones Biológicas del Noreste, México
Francisco Javier Hernández López	Centro de Investigaciones en Matemáticas, México
Jean-Bernard Hayet	Centro de Investigaciones en Matemáticas, México
Nidiyare Hevia-Montiel	IIMAS-UNAM, México
Szymon Jaroszewicz	Polish Academy of Sciences, Poland
Ricardo Legarda Sáenz	Universidad Autónoma de Yucatán, México
Stacey Levine	Duquesne University, USA
Elena Loli Piccolomini	University of Bologna, Italy
José Luis López Martínez	Universidad Autónoma de Yucatán, México
Sven Magg	Hamburg Universität, Germany
Francisco Madera	Universidad Autónoma de Yucatán, México
Israel Martínez	CICESE, México
Anabel Martin-Gonzalez	Universidad Autónoma de Yucatán, México
Elena Martínez Pérez	IIMAS-UNAM, México

Rolando Medellín	University of Essex, UK
Jan Hendrik Metzen	Deutsche Forschungszentrum für Künstliche Intelligenz, Germany
Eric Molino-Minero-Re	IIMAS-UNAM, México
Dagmar Monett	Berlin School of Economics and Law, Germany
Raúl Monroy Borja	ITESM-CEM, México
Francisco Moo-Mena	Universidad Autónoma de Yucatán, México
Jaime Ortegón Silverio	Universidad de Quintana Roo, México
Karinne Ramírez Amaro	Technische Universität München, Germany
Jorge Ríos Martínez	Universidad Autónoma de Yucatán, México
Eduardo Rodríguez-Martínez	Universidad Autónoma Metropolitana, México
Asad Safi	Institute of Information Technology, Pakistan
Israel Sánchez Domínguez	IIMAS-UNAM, México
Ahmad Shahid	Institute of Information Technology, Pakistan
Victor Uc-Cetina	Universidad Autónoma de Yucatán, México
Andrez Vasquez	CINVESTAV-Guadalajara, México
Flavio Vigueras Gómez	Universidad Autónoma de San Luis Potosí, México
Yalin Zheng	University of Liverpool, UK
Sheikh Ziauddin	Institute of Information Technology, Pakistan

Organizing Committee

Anabel Martin-Gonzalez	Universidad Autónoma de Yucatán, México
Víctor Uc-Cetina	Universidad Autónoma de Yucatán, México
Jose V. Alcala-Burgos	Centro de Investigaciones en Matemáticas, México
Carlos Brito-Loeza	Universidad Autónoma de Yucatán, México
Nidiyare Hevia-Montiel	IIMAS-UNAM, México

Contents

Optimization of the Dictionary Size Selection: An Efficient Combination of K-SVD and PCA to Denoise and Enhance Digital Mammography Contrast

Sègbédji R.T.J. Goubalan[1,2(✉)], Khalifa Djemal[2], and Hichem Maaref[2]

[1] École Polytechnique de Montréal, Université de Montréal, Montréal, Canada
`segbedji-rethice-theophile-j.goubalan@polymtl.ca`
[2] Laboratoire IBISC, Université d'Evry Val d'Essonne, Evry, France
{`Junior.Goubalan,Khalifa.Djemal,Hichem.Maaref`}`@ibisc.univ-evry.fr`

Abstract. Mammographic images are often characterized by a low contrast and a relatively high noise content, due to 3-D breast structures projection onto a 2-D image plane. These effects may hinder lesion detection. During the past decade, many techniques have been proposed to improve the mammography contrast. Nevertheless, some image regions might not be adequately enhanced, while others might be subjected to excessive enhancement. For that reason, we propose a method to denoise the images and enhance contrast uniformly. First, we used a machine learning method to create a sparse dictionary from the database, then we used the principal component analysis to reduce the size of the dictionary before decoding each patch of a given mammography. Finally, the algorithm was tested on MIAS and INbreast databases using the same parameters' values for each image. The results show that the visibility of breast mass and anatomic detail were considerably improved compared to the wavelet method and the computation time is halved compared to the conventional sparse coding algorithm and the curvelet method.

Keywords: Digital mammography · Denoising · Contrast enhancement · Sparse dictionary learning · Principal component analysis

1   Introduction

Breast cancer is among the leading causes of cancer deaths for women. In 2012, 522 000 deaths have been recorded worldwide, representing a 14 % increase compared to 2008 [1]. Early diagnosis and treatment can improve survival rates among patients suffering from breast cancer [2]. Despite the emergence of digital breast tomosynthesis (DBT), mammography is still the only recognized screening exam used in the clinic, because it allows for cancer detection at early stages, therefore reducing the mortality rate [3].

© Springer International Publishing Switzerland 2016
A. Martin-Gonzalez and V. Uc-Cetina (Eds.): ISICS 2016, CCIS 597, pp. 1–15, 2016.
DOI: 10.1007/978-3-319-30447-2_1

In 2-D mammography, image interpretation by radiologists is difficult, time-consuming, and sometimes increases the ratio of false positives due to tissue superimposition. This is even more apparent in the context of screening exams, because decisions that pose a threat to the patient's life should be avoided. Some studies have shown that the preprocessed images allow the detection of more true masses in the mammographies and improve the accuracy of their segmentation [4]. Hence, to help radiologists improve detection and diagnosis accuracy, all while facilitating further steps of the computer-aided detection (CAD) system, several denoising and contrast enhancement techniques have been proposed and tested. A recent review of those contributions can be found in [5,6]. Among the methods exposed in this paper, there are three classes of preprocessing techniques of mammographic images: global transformations for contrast enhancement, adaptative contrast enhancement algorithms and methods for nonlinear contrast enhancement and the wavelet-based approach.

Histogram equalization (HE) is one method of the first class. It yields poor results, because it fails to adapt to the variability in size and shape of the structures contained within the mammography. Moreover, it emphasizes the noise in the images which are often already noisy. Adaptative neighborhood contrast enhancement (ANCE) [7], which improves the contrast by taking into account each image pixel's neighborhood, was an alternative to the global transformations for a long time, before the emergence of techniques based on multi-resolution representation. The dyadic wavelet transform [8,9] belongs to the latter. These methods vary depending on the mother wavelet formulation and the coefficients used. Similarly, the curvelet transform is used in various image processing techniques, including denoising. It is a non-adaptive technique for multi-scale object representation. As an extension of the wavelet concept, it encodes directional information with precision that increases as the scale refines [10,11]. These methods work similarly to a band-pass filter and improve the contrast of different lesions regardless of the size and type of the anatomical structures.

Even using these advanced techniques, the image quality remains unsatisfactory because the methods induce non-negligible bias. Thus, we propose a preprocessing method in the aim of providing an effective solution which reduces image bias. It is based on the learning of a sparse dictionary (LSD) from the database, done by the K-singular value decomposition (K-SVD) algorithm [12]. Due to the empirical nature of the choice of dictionary size and its impact in the computation time (CTe) required for noise reduction in an image, we use principal component analysis (PCA) to significantly reduce the dimension of the dictionary. Then each patch of the noisy image is decoded on the reduced dictionary before histogram normalization.

The images obtained after denoising and contrast enhancement neither exposed noise amplification more distorted the anatomical structure present in the mammography. Consequently, the result maintained the familiar appearance of the original mammogram with excellent visual quality, compared to Daubechies wavelets [13], and using a lower computation time than the conventional K-SVD method. The performance of the proposed method was evaluated via the peak signal to noise ratio (PSNR), mean square error (MSE) and the CTe. In Sect. 2 of this paper, our algorithm of mammographic image denoising and contrast enhancement is presented in detail. The experimental results are exposed and discussed in Sect. 5 followed by the conclusion in Sect. 6.

2   Methodology

2.1   Patch Extraction and Pre-processing

Firstly, several square image regions called *patches* denoted as p of size $s \times s$ pixels were extracted from random locations within each region of interest (ROI). The ROIs were selected according to the ground truth lesion margins provided by the radiologists. These patches were allowed to intersect. Then, the patches were centered (1) and normalized (2) as illustrated in Fig. 1, with $p(x, y)$ the intensity value of a pixel located in the patch p at the position given by coordinates x and y.

$$p'(x,y) = p(x,y) - \bar{p}, \quad \text{with } \bar{p} = \frac{1}{s^2}\sum_{x=1}^{s}\sum_{y=1}^{s} p(x,y). \tag{1}$$

$$p''(x,y) = \frac{p'(x,y)}{\|\, p'\,\|_2}, \quad \text{with } \|\, p'\,\|_2 = \sqrt{\sum_{x=1}^{s}\sum_{y=1}^{s} p'(x,y)^2}. \tag{2}$$

2.2   Learning Sparse Dictionary and K-SVD Algorithm

K-SVD is an algorithm for adapting dictionaries in order to achieve a sparse image representation. Given a set of training images, we seek the dictionary that leads to the best representation for each member in this set, while imposing strict sparsity constraints. It generalizes the K-means clustering process [12].

Let N designate the number of patches extracted from the image. Let the set of patches be designated as $\{y_i\}_{i \in \{1;N\}}$, with each patch vectorized as $y_i \in \mathbb{R}^n$, $n = s^2$ and $\mathbf{Y}_{n \times N}$ a matrix where y_i is a column vector. $\mathbf{Y}$ is to be represented as a linear combination $\mathbf{X}$ of basis elements denoted $\mathbf{D}$:

$$\mathbf{Y} \approx \mathbf{DX}. \tag{3}$$

$\mathbf{D}_{n \times K}$ is a matrix whose column vectors are the K elements of the dictionary which is being learned. $\mathbf{X}_{K \times N}$ is the matrix whose row vectors $\{x_k\}_{k \in \{1;N\}}$ contain all the projections of $\mathbf{Y}$ in $\mathbf{D}$. In order to get the best representation of patch data $\mathbf{Y}$, the problem is to find $\mathbf{D}$ and $\mathbf{X}$ minimizing the criterion below:

$$\min_{\mathbf{D},\mathbf{X}}\{\|\, \mathbf{Y} - \mathbf{DX}\,\|_2^2\}. \tag{4}$$

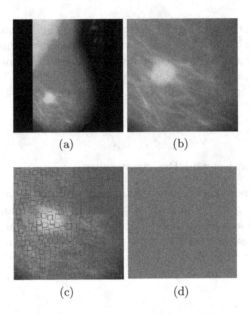

(a) (b)

(c)   (d)

Fig. 1. Patch extraction and pre-processing steps: (a) original image. (b) lesion ROI. (c) patch extraction on ROI, with 5x zoom in insert, and (d) normalized patches.

$\| \mathbf{X} \|_2$ is the L_2-norm defined as $\sqrt{\sum_{ij} \mathbf{X}_{ij}^2}$. If $n < K$, then $\mathbf{D}$ is a full rank matrix, which means that an infinite number of solutions exist. Imposing constraints will limit the search space. Notably, constraints restricting the projection $\boldsymbol{y}_i$ on the dictionary $\mathbf{D}$ using sparse coding have been much studied [14]. Therefore one could solve the following problem:

$$\min_{\mathbf{D},\mathbf{X}}\{\| \mathbf{Y} - \mathbf{DX} \|_2^2\}, \quad \text{subject to} : \ \forall i \ \| \boldsymbol{x}_i \|_0 \leq T_0. \qquad (5)$$

$\| \boldsymbol{x}_i \|_0$ is the L_0-norm of vector $\boldsymbol{x}_i$ i.e. the number of its nonzero components, and T_0 the sparsity level (number of nonzero entries) which is to be determined empirically.

To solve the LSD problem described in (5), we used the optimized K-SVD algorithm [12,15]. The K-SVD algorithm consists of an alternating optimization. First, it iteratively solves a partial problem in $\mathbf{X}$ with $\mathbf{D}$ fixed: this is the *Sparse Coding* step in which we solve:

$$\min_{\mathbf{X}}\{\| \mathbf{Y} - \mathbf{DX} \|_2^2\}, \quad \text{subject to} : \ \forall i \in \{1; N\} \ \| \boldsymbol{x}_i \|_0 \leq T_0. \qquad (6)$$

Many techniques exist to solve (6), in our case the orthogonal matching pursuit (OMP) [16,17] was selected. It is greedy and not optimal; nevertheless, it has interesting properties regarding error reduction between the original and the sparse dictionary.

The second step of the K-SVD algorithm consists in optimizing $\mathbf{D}$ with $\mathbf{X}$ fixed. Thus we have:

$$\min_{\mathbf{D}}\{\| \mathbf{Y} - \mathbf{DX} \|_2^2\}. \tag{7}$$

This involves a successive optimization of each element d_k of the dictionary, independently of the other elements, the latter being assumed fixed. The cost function (7) can be rewritten as:

$$f(\mathbf{D}) = \| \mathbf{Y} - \mathbf{DX} \|_2^2 = \left\| \mathbf{Y} - \sum_{j=1}^{K} d_j x_T^j \right\|_2^2 = \left\| \left(\mathbf{Y} - \sum_{j \neq k}^{K} d_j x_T^j \right) - d_k x_T^k \right\|_2^2$$

$$= \left\| E_k - d_k x_T^k \right\|_2^2. \tag{8}$$

with d_k a column of the dictionary $\mathbf{D}$, and the coefficients x_T^k corresponding to the kth row in $\mathbf{X}$. Note that x_T^k is not equivalent to x_k, the latter being the kth column of $\mathbf{X}$. Each product $d_j x_T^j$ is a matrix of size $(n \times N)$. The term E_k in (8) is the reconstruction error with regard to patch data, for an optimization performed with K-1 elements in the dictionary $\{d_j\}_{j \neq k}$.

As these elements are assumed fixed, $f(d_k)$ is to be minimized. It is possible to minimize $f(d_k)$ by the least squares method, but it should be ensured that the solution update always allows for a sparse decomposition. To ensure this property, specific weights are defined:

$$w_k = \{i | 1 \leq i \leq K, x_T^k(i) \neq 0\}. \tag{9}$$

where w_k is the set index for the samples $\mathbf{Y} = \{y_i\}$ which use the element d_k. The method used to optimize d_k is:

1. Restrict E_k by choosing only the columns corresponding to w_k and get E_k^R. We denote $\mathbf{\Omega_k}$ the matrix of size $N \times | w_k |$ which corresponds to copy N times the row vector w_k, so $E_k^R = E_k \mathbf{\Omega_k}$ and $x_R^k = x_T^k \mathbf{\Omega_k}$,

2. The solution consists of minimizing $\left\| E_k^R - d_k x_R^k \right\|_2^2$ with respect to both d_k and x_R^k by ensuring that the support of x_T^k (i.e. nonzero w_k) remains unchanged. To determine $\min_{d_k, x_R^k} \left\| E_k^R - d_k x_R^k \right\|_2^2$ we used the SVD algorithm on the cost function $E_k^R = \mathbf{U \Delta V^T}$. The solution for d_k and x_R^k is:

(a) d_k is the first column of $\mathbf{U}$ (unitary matrix),
(b) x_R^k is the first column of $\mathbf{V}$ (unitary matrix) multiplied by $\mathbf{\Delta}(1,1)$ (diagonal matrix).

We applied this algorithm to the patches' databases, obtained as explained in Sect. 2.1. Figure 2 shows the results obtained using one database.

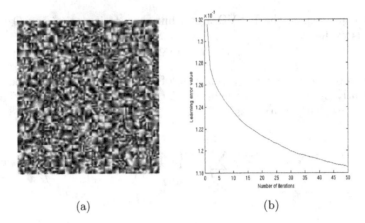

(a)   (b)

Fig. 2. Learning of sparse dictionary: (a) codebook learned on patches database and (b) learning error graph. Note the monotonically decreasing learning error in (b).

2.3   Dictionary Dimension Reduction: PCA

PCA is a well-known algorithm for dimensionality reduction and feature extraction [18], which attempts to find a linear subspace of lower dimension than the original feature space, where the new components have the largest variance. In our case, the size of the previously learned dictionary varies depending on the user and there is no way to control its size. A larger dictionary induces higher computation times. Then, a new approach to reduce the computation time by searching the most important patches was developed in this work.

Consider the dictionary $\mathbf{D}\{d_k\}_{k\in\{1;L\}}$, where L is the size of the sparse dictionary and d_k is a patch of size $s \times s$, which is considered to be a vector of dimension s^2. Thus, the set of patches maps to a collection of points in a large space. The patches are similar in overall configuration, due to the repetitive patterns often found in mammography, the so-called *Tabar patches* [19]. They are not uniformly distributed in this large space and thereby can be described by a subspace with fewer dimensions. The main idea of the PCA method is to find the subset of patches that best account for the overall distribution of the patches in the dictionary.

The dictionary is then subject to PCA, which seeks a set of M orthogonal vectors $(M < L)$ which best describe the distribution of the data. It is assumed that the projection is denoted as $\mathbf{Z} = \mathbf{AD}$ where $\mathbf{A} = [u_1{}^T, ..., u_M{}^T]$, and $u_i{}^T u_i = 1$ for $i \in \{1; M\}$. The variance of $\mathbf{Z}\{z_k\}_{k\in\{1;L\}}$, which is the trace of the covariance matrix of $\mathbf{Z}$, is to be maximized. Thus, the resulting cost function is:

$$\mathbf{Z}^* = \underset{\mathbf{Z}}{\mathrm{argmax}}\ \mathrm{tr}\ (\mathbf{C_Z}). \tag{10}$$

where

$$\mathbf{C_Z} = \frac{1}{L}\sum_{k=1}^{L}(z_k - \bar{\mathbf{Z}})(z_k - \bar{\mathbf{Z}})^T. \tag{11}$$

and

$$\bar{\mathbf{Z}} = \frac{1}{L} \sum_{k=1}^{L} d_k. \tag{12}$$

Let $\mathbf{C_D}$ be the covariance matrix of $\mathbf{D}$. Since, $\mathrm{tr}(\mathbf{C_Z}) = \mathrm{tr}(\mathbf{AC_Z A}^T)$. By using the lagrangian multipliers, denoted by λ_i, the following expression will be maximized for each i:

$$u_i{}^T \mathbf{C_Z} u_i + \lambda_i (1 - u_i{}^T u_i). \tag{13}$$

By setting the derivative with respect to u_i equal to zero, we can observe that (13) will have a stationary point if:

$$\mathbf{C_Z} u_i = \lambda_i u_i. \tag{14}$$

which means that u_i is an eigenvector of $\mathbf{C_D}$. If we left-multiply each side of (14) by $u_i{}^T$ and use the remarkable property that $u_i{}^T u_i = 1$, we note that the variance is given by:

$$u_i{}^T \mathbf{C_Z} u_i = \lambda_i. \tag{15}$$

Thus, d_k can be represented as:

$$d_k = \sum_{k=1}^{L} (d_k{}^T u_i) u_i. \tag{16}$$

Note that d_k can be also approximated by:

$$\hat{d}_k = \sum_{k=1}^{M} (d_k{}^T u_i) u_i. \tag{17}$$

where u_i is the eigenvector of $\mathbf{C_D}$ corresponding to the ith largest eigenvalue.

2.4   Denoising and Contrast Enhancement

In this paper, numerical simulation was used to obtain noisy input images; namely, additive gaussian noise was applied. To denoise and enhance the mammography contrast, machine learning of a dictionary was performed on each database. Once the dictionary dimension was reduced, it was used to denoise each patch y_i. The denoising method consists of decoding each noisy patch from within the dictionary, i.e. determining optimal projection $\hat{x}$ so as to minimize:

$$\hat{x} = \min_{x_i} \| x_i \|_0, \quad \text{subject to} \ : \ \| \mathbf{Y} - \mathbf{DX} \|_2^2 \leq \Gamma_0. \tag{18}$$

Opposite to the classical sparse coding, the approach is not an attempt to reconstruct exactly the patch y_i, which is noisy. Instead, a reasonable threshold ($\leq \Gamma_0$) is sought.

3   Materials

We tested the proposed denoising and contrast enhancement method on two databases: the well-known MIAS database [20] and the INbreast database [21]. The first one was provided by the Mammographic Image Analysis Society (MIAS) in the UK. It consists of 161 cases, 322 digitized mediolateral oblique (MLO) images with a resolution of 50 microns and an image matrix of 1024×1024 pixels. It contains several types of findings, including benign and malign lesions and normal images.

The second database was acquired in Portugal between April 2008 and July 2010 with MammoNovation Siemens full-filled digital mammography (FFDM) equipment. The pixel size was of 70 microns, the image grayscale depth was 14-bit, the image matrix was of either 3328×4084 pixels or 2560×3328 pixels, depending on the compression plate used for the acquisition, according to the patient breast size. It contained a total of 115 cases, with 90 cases having two images of each breast: MLO and craniocaudal (CC). The 25 remaining cases were of women who had a mastectomy and two views of only one breast were included, for a total of 410 images.

The ground truth images given by radiologists were used to crop the area where the breast mass was located. In this manner, image databases which were only composed of ROIs were obtained, and the presented technique was applied on the latter.

4   Numerical Implementation

The ROIs obtained above were rescaled to the same grid size of 300×300 pixels in the aim to extract the same number of patches from each image. The rescaling was performed via bicubic interpolation. Then, 20000 patches of size $s \times s$ (on each database) were extracted with $s=14$ and $\delta=6$ was selected as the maximum intersection area between two patches. To produce the dictionary on each database, we used the following parameters: a dictionary size of 500 patches, a sparsity level of 10 nonzero entries, and a number of iterations of 50.

To generate the gaussian noise (GN) in the image, a standard deviation $\sigma = 20$ was used. This value was estimated according to generally accepted mammogram acquisition parameters. The uncertainty due to quantum noise was considered for two illustrative cases: a typical film acquisition, with $50\,\mu$Gy air Kerma (kinetic energy released per unit mass) at the surface of the detector and a detective quantum efficiency (DQE) of 0.35, and a low-dose digital mammography acquisition, with $35\,\mu$Gy air Kerma and a detector DQE of 0.5, as suggested by the findings of Monnin et al. [22]. Exponential attenuation of 17.5 keV photons in 4 cm of compressed breast tissue [23] and a total of 2 cm of tissue-equivalent compression plates was considered. The relative standard deviation of the pixel values was estimated in these conditions. It yielded 15 % in both cases. This corresponds to $\sigma = 20$ for the 8-bit grayscale images, where the maximum breast radiodensity was represented by pixel values of about 133.

In order to perform the comparison between our approach and the Daubechies wavelet, we used the MATLAB® (2014a) wavelet toolbox with these parameters: wname=db10, level of decomposition=3, thresholds (horizontal/diagonal/vertical coefficients)=4/4/8 (the same for three levels). For the comparison with curvelet, we used the toolbox provide by authors and available in [24]. For each image, we applied unequally-spaced fast Fourier transform (USFFT), which uses a decimated rectangular grid tilted along the main direction of each curvelet. There is one such grid per scale and angle.

To enhance the image contrast with both LSD and our method (LSD-PCA) the following threshold was used: $\Gamma_0 = s \times \sigma \times$ bias, with bias $= 1.15$, the latter being found empirically after multiple trials.

In order to provide a proof of the efficiency of our method, we computed the PSNR and the MSE metrics. Let I_s the original image, I_r the reconstruted image, N_r, M_c and d respectively the number of rows and columns of the image, and the image grey level intensity range. Thus,

$$\text{PSNR}(I_r, I_s) = 10 \log_{10} \left(\frac{d^2}{\text{MSE}(I_r, I_s)} \right). \tag{19}$$

with

$$\text{MSE}(I_r, I_s) = \frac{1}{N_r \times M_c} \sum_{i=1}^{N_r} \sum_{j=1}^{M_c} [I_r(i,j) - I_s(i,j)]^2. \tag{20}$$

The purpose of the PSNR is to quantitatively assess our method, with higher PSNR indicating higher image quality. Even though the MSE is closely related to the PSNR, both metrics are reported for the reader's convenience.

5   Results and Discussion

5.1   Application on ROIs

The use of PCA has allowed for the reduction of the dictionary size from 500 patches to 40, which represents a 12.5 × dictionary size reduction. Figure 3 below provides an overview of the distribution of eigenvalues computed for the PCA. It demonstrates that only 8 % of data from our original dictionary represent more than 99.99 % of information contained in our database. This result confirms the initial hypothesis that mammographic patches are very similar.

To evaluate the quality of our approach, it was compared to one of the most common denoising techniques in mammography, the Daubechies wavelet [13] method. It was also compared to the theoretically similar, but highly refined curvelet method [11]. The latter two are well-known in image denoising and are similarly parametrized via image decomposition levels and threshold values. Finally, the current approach was compared to the conventional LSD algorithm. The results are shown in Figs. 4 and 5. The differences between the images before and after noise suppression are evident: for lesion ROIs, it can be noted that the images (c), (d) and (f) of Fig. 4 and (c), (d) and (f) Fig. 5 are blurred compared

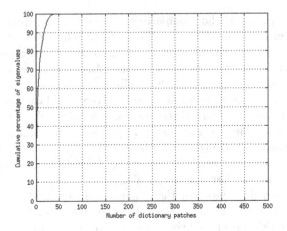

Fig. 3. Cumulative percentage of eigenvalues.

to the corresponding ground-truth images. However, in Figs. 4(e) and 5(e), one may observe that most of the added noise subsists in the image filtered via the Daubechies wavelet approach. In contrast, the curvelet method effectively suppressed noise, at the cost of an added blurring and artifacts, which are more or less important in the different regions of the image in Figs. 4(f) and 5(f). In the same way, we can observe that LSD, shown in Figs. 4(c), 5(c) and LSD-PCA, shown in Figs. 4(d) and 5(d) seem to suffer from blurring, but they remove as much noise as curvelet approach, while avoiding introducing artifacts in the image. Moreover, one may easily notice that LSD and LSD-PCA respond well to the histogram normalization, unlike the curvelet method.

The PSNR metric was used to quantitatively confirm the visual results above. PSNR values of (24.61 ± 0.05) dB versus (38.80 ± 1.5) dB were observed for MIAS, and (24.62 ± 0.04) dB vs (39.01 ± 1.39) dB for INbreast, using Daubechies wavelets and the curvelet method, respectively. Also, (37.87 ± 1.97) dB versus (37.91 ± 1.73) dB were observed for MIAS, and (37.55 ± 2.06) dB vs (37.56 ± 1.96) dB for INbreast, using the LSD and LSD-PCA techniques, respectively. These results, reported in Tables 1 and 2 along with the MSE values, show that our approach and two others – LSD and curvelet, are more efficient than the Daubechies wavelet method for the current application. It is important to mention that the Daubechies and curvelet methods require a careful selection of the decomposition levels and thresholds, while the LSD and LSD-PCA do not require such operations. Furthermore, these mean PSNR values show that LSD, LSD-PCA and curvelet methods demonstrate a similar capability with regard to image reconstruction, with a slight advantage for the curvelet method. Specifically, the mean absolute gap in PSNR between the curvelet and the dictionary-based methods is of 1.17 dB. It is important to note that considering the dynamic range of 8-bit images, the maximum PSNR of an image is of 48.13 dB. The efficiency of LSD and LSD-PCA techniques is based on the

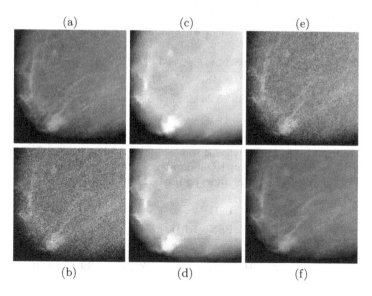

Fig. 4. Comparison of four methods to remove the noise and enhance the contrast with an image provided by MIAS: (a) ROI, (b) GN, (c) LSD, (d) LSD-PCA, (e) Daubechies and (f) curvelet.

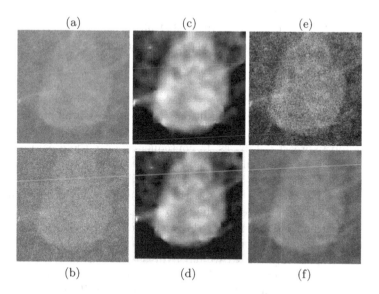

Fig. 5. Comparison of four methods to remove the noise and enhance the contrast with an image provided by INbreast: (a) ROI, (b) GN, (c) LSD, (d) LSD-PCA, (e) Daubechies and (f) curvelet.

Table 1. Mean and standard deviation values of the MSE metric on MIAS (322 images) and INbreast (410 images) ROIs databases after application of Daubechies, LSD, LSD-PCA and Curvelet algorithms on images with numerically added noise.

	Daubechies	LSD	LSD-PCA	Curvelet
	MSE	MSE	MSE	MSE
MIAS	62.10±0.40	5.70±2.87	5.68±2.75	**4.01±1.26**
INbreast	61.91±0.53	6.08±2.80	6.08±2.78	**4.02±1.38**

Table 2. Mean and standard deviation values of the PSNR metric on MIAS (322 images) and INbreast (410 images) ROIs databases after application of Daubechies, LSD, LSD-PCA and Curvelet algorithms on images with numerically added noise.

	Daubechies	LSD	LSD-PCA	Curvelet
	PSNR (dB)	PSNR (dB)	PSNR (dB)	PSNR (dB)
MIAS	24.61±0.05	37.87±1.97	37.91±1.73	**38.80±1.5**
INbreast	24.62±0.04	37.55±2.06	37.56±1.96	**39.01±1.39**

Table 3. Mean and standard deviation values of CTe measure on MIAS (322 images) and INbreast (410 images) ROIs databases after application of Daubechies, LSD, LSD-PCA and Curvelet algorithms on images with numerically added noise.

	Daubechies	LSD	LSD-PCA	Curvelet
	CTe (s)	CTe (s)	CTe (s)	CTe (s)
MIAS	0.15±0.06	3.70±0.23	**1.65±0.19**	3.76±0.15
INbreast	0.26±0.10	3.84±0.21	**1.77±0.18**	3.76±0.19

fact that they assume that image noise prevents sparse decomposition, due to the random nature of the noise. In addition, an appropriate level of sparsity was determined for each database, which improved the quality of all images from both MIAS and INbreast databases. In consequence, once these parameters are fixed, the LSD-PCA algorithm may be interpreted as automatic. This allows one to avoid the hassle of selecting the number of levels of decomposition and the thresholds values for each image in the databases, which occurs when the Daubechies wavelet and curvelet methods are used.

The computation time was evaluated as well, see Table 3. For the Daubechies wavelet method, the computation times (CTe) were of (0.15±0.06) s and (0.26±0.10) s, respectively, for MIAS and INbreast databases. Whereas, for the curvelet method, the CTe were of (3.76±0.15) s and (3.76±0.19) s, respectively. LSD yielded (3.70±0.23) s and (3.84±0.21) s, respectively. The latter two times are about an order of magnitude higher than for the wavelet method. The LSD-PCA method presented in this work is about 2× faster than LSD and curvelet methods, with (1.65±0.19) s and (1.77±0.18) s respectively. Nevertheless,

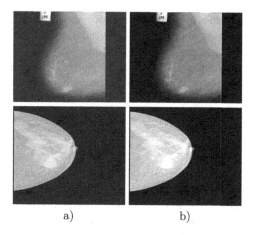

Fig. 6. Mammographies denoising and enhancement with upper image provided by MIAS and the image below obtained by INbreast: (a) original images without noise and (b) results after application of LSD-PCA algorithm.

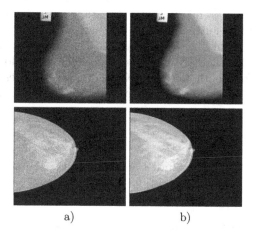

Fig. 7. Mammographies denoising and enhancement with upper image provided by MIAS and the image below obtained by INbreast: (a) original images with noise and (b) results after application of LSD-PCA algorithm.

LSD-PCA cannot reach the low computation times of the Daubechies method. From a more general perspective, it is remarkable that the LSD-PCA method is capable of achieving denoising levels and contrast enhancement comparable to state-of-the-art algorithms, but requiring only half the computation time.

5.2 Extension to Full Mammographies

The dictionary learned from each database was also used to attempt to denoise each full mammography. In addition, the results of the application of LSD-PCA on images without numerically added noise are shown in Fig. 6. These images demonstrate higher contrast and a reduction of acquisition noise. Figure 7 shows the result we obtained for raw mammographies with added noise. One can note that even when using the limited-size dictionary learned on a few patches extracted from any database, the entire mammography can be reconstructed almost perfectly via LSD-PCA, even if the image is corrupted by noise.

6   Conclusion

This paper proposed a denoising and contrast enhancement algorithm based on LSD and PCA. The original contribution is based on the reduction of the dimensionality of the dictionary learned from the database. The proposed LSD-PCA method demonstrated excellent visual quality and a uniform enhancement of the contrast, while preserving the appearance of the anatomical structures present in the mammography. The algorithm outperformed the Daubechies wavelet method in terms of image quality, but required a significantly longer computation time. It performed similarly to the conventional LSD and the curvelet methods with regard to of image quality, while reconstruction time was reduced twice compared to these two techniques. Furthermore, it was shown to denoise and enhance the contrast of mammographies with the same parameters' values for two different image databases (MIAS and INbreast), and optimal thresholds were found for images originating from both databases. Considering all the results presented in this paper, LSD-PCA seems fit for potential clinical application.

References

1. IARC. Globocan 2012: Estimatied Cancer Incidence, Mortality and Prevalence Worldwide in 2012 (2012). http://globocan.iarc.fr/Default.aspx
2. Cady, B., Michaelson, J.S.: The life-sparing potential of mammographic screening. Cancer **91**(9), 1699–1703 (2001)
3. Elmore, J.G., Armstrong, K., Lehman, C.D., Fletcher, S.W.: Screening for breast cancer. Jama **293**(10), 1245–1256 (2005)
4. Li, H., Wang, Y., Liu, K.J., Lo, S.-C.B., Freedman, M.T.: Computerized radiographic mass detection-Part I: lesion site selection by morphological enhancement and contextual segmentation. IEEE Trans. Med. Imaging **20**(4), 289–301 (2001)
5. Rangayyan, R.M., Ayres, F.J., Leo Desautels, J.E.: A review of computer-aided diagnosis of breast cancer: toward the detection of subtle signs. J. Franklin Inst. **344**(3), 312–348 (2007)
6. Ganesan, K., Acharya, U.R., Chua, C.K., Min, L.C., Abraham, K.T., Ng, K.-H.: Computer-aided breast cancer detection using mammograms: a review. IEEE Rev. Biomed. Eng. **6**, 77–98 (2013)
7. Gordon, R., Rangayyan, R.M.: Feature enhancement of film mammograms using fixed and adaptive neighborhoods. Appl. Opt. **23**(4), 560–564 (1984). Optical Society of America
8. Laine, A.F., Schuler, S., Fan, J., Huda, W.: Mammographic feature enhancement by multiscale analysis. IEEE Trans. Med. Imaging **13**(4), 725–740 (1994)

9. Mencattini, A., Salmeri, M., Lojacono, R., Frigerio, M., Caselli, F.: Mammographic images enhancement and denoising for breast cancer detection using dyadic wavelet processing. IEEE Trans. Instrum. Meas. **57**(7), 1422–1430 (2008)
10. Candes, E.J., Donoho, D.L.: Curvelets, multiresolution representation, and scaling laws. In: International Symposium on Optical Science and Technology, pp. 1–12. International Society for Optics and Photonics (2000)
11. Candes, E.J., Demanet, L., Donoho, D.L., Ying, L.: Fast discrete curvelet transforms. Multiscale Model. Simul. **5**(3), 861–899 (2006)
12. Aharon, M., Elad, M., Bruckstein, A.: K-svd: an algorithm for designing overcomplete dictionaries for sparse representation. IEEE Trans. Sig. Process. **54**(11), 4311–4322 (2006)
13. Daubechies, I., et al.: Ten Lectures on Wavelets. vol. 61. SIAM (1992)
14. Chen, S., Billings, S.A., Luo, W.: Orthogonal least squares methods and their application to non-linear system identification. Int. J. Control **50**(5), 1873–1896 (1989)
15. Rubinstein, R., Zibulevsky, M., Elad, M.: Double sparsity: learning sparse dictionaries for sparse signal approximation. IEEE Trans. Sig. Process. **58**(3), 1553–1564 (2010)
16. Davis, G.M., Mallat, S.G., Zhang, Z.: Adaptive time-frequency decompositions. Opt. Eng. **33**(7), 2183–2191 (1994)
17. Tropp, J.A.: Greed is good: algorithmic results for sparse approximation. IEEE Trans. Inf. Theor. **50**(10), 2231–2242 (2004)
18. Kirby, M., Sirovich, L.: Application of the karhunen-loeve procedure for the characterization of human faces. IEEE Trans. Pattern Anal. Mach. Intell. **12**(1), 03–108 (1990)
19. Tabár, L., Tot, T., Dean, P.B.: Breast cancer: the art and science of early detection with mammography: perception, interpretation, histopathologic correlation. Georg Thieme Verlag (2004)
20. Suckling, J., Parker, J., Dance, D.R., Astley, S., Hunt, J., Doggis, C.R.M., Ricketts, I., Stamatakis, E., Cerneaz, N., Kok, S.L., Taylor, P., Betal, D., Savage, J.: The mammographic image analysis society digital mammogram database. In: Exerpta Medica. International Congress Series, vol. 1069, pp. 375–378 (1994)
21. Moreira, I.C., Amaral, I., Domingues, I., Cardoso, A., Cardoso, M.J., Cardoso, J.S.: Inbreast: toward a full-field digital mammographic database. Acad. Radiol. **19**(2), 236–248 (2012)
22. Monnin, P., Gutierrez, D., Bulling, S., Guntern, D., Verdun, F.R.: A comparison of the performance of digital mammography systems. Med. Phys. **34**(3), 906–914 (2007)
23. Poulos, A., McLean, D., Richard, M., Heard, R.: Breast compression in mammography: how much is enough? Australas. Radiol. **47**(2), 121–126 (2003)
24. Candes, E.J.: CurveLab-2.1.3 (2012). http://www.curvelet.org/index.html

Robustness of Deep Convolutional Neural Networks for Image Recognition

Matej Uličný[(✉)], Jens Lundström, and Stefan Byttner

Intelligent Systems Department, Halmstad University,
Box 823, S301 18 Halmstad, Sweden
mtj.ulicny@gmail.com, {jens.lundstrom,stefan.byttner}@hh.se
http://hh.se/ite

Abstract. Recent research has found deep neural networks to be vulnerable, by means of prediction error, to images corrupted by small amounts of non-random noise. These images, known as adversarial examples are created by exploiting the input to output mapping of the network. For the MNIST database, we observe in this paper how well the known regularization/robustness methods improve generalization performance of deep neural networks when classifying adversarial examples and examples perturbed with random noise. We conduct a comparison of these methods with our proposed robustness method, an ensemble of models trained on adversarial examples, able to clearly reduce prediction error. Apart from robustness experiments, human classification accuracy for adversarial examples and examples perturbed with random noise is measured. Obtained human classification accuracy is compared to the accuracy of deep neural networks measured in the same experimental settings. The results indicate, human performance does not suffer from neural network adversarial noise.

Keywords: Adversarial examples · Deep neural network · Noise robustness

1 Introduction

In visual recognition problems, deep neural networks (DNN's) represent the state-of-the-art models outperforming all the other machine learning algorithms. The use of neural networks for visual recognition has application in many fields, from web applications to industrial products such as safeguards in automobile industry. Despite their outstanding performance, they have pitfalls in their understanding of problem they are trained to solve. Szegedy et al. have discovered robustness flaws in many machine learning methods [11]. Despite the fact that the most of machine learning methods exhibit these flaws, this article specializes exclusively on deep neural networks. Deep neural networks have problems to correctly classify images altered by non-random noise, imperceptibly different from images that have been classified correctly. Such flaw is unacceptable if neural networks are used for safety protocols or for verification programs.

© Springer International Publishing Switzerland 2016
A. Martin-Gonzalez and V. Uc-Cetina (Eds.): ISICS 2016, CCIS 597, pp. 16–30, 2016.
DOI: 10.1007/978-3-319-30447-2_2

In this work we define robustness as the ability to correctly classify similar inputs. Without a robust solution, attacker is able to create examples that can perturb the network.

We approach the problem by testing several robustness methods and by comparing their results. The article provides investigation of robustness not only to adversarial noise, but also to random noise. All experiments are performed on the MNIST [8] data-set. Different approaches, such as various configurations of dropout or pre-processing the input are examined. Robustness experiments are finalized with a study of adversarial training and robustness of various types of committees.

Several articles report human visual recognition accuracy on certain data-sets [1, 12]. We provide an estimate of human perception ability on noisy MNIST images and we compare it to the accuracy of deep neural networks.

The paper is organized as follows, Sect. 2 presents an outline of a related work in the field. Perturbations and robustness methods we use in experiments are briefly described in Sect. 3. Method description is followed by experimental setup (Sect. 4) and results of the experiments (Sect. 5). The paper is finalized by the main conclusions and by a discussion of their aspects (Sect. 6).

2 Related Work

Recent discoveries by Szegedy et al. [11] opened a whole new branch for research of DNNs. Instead of describing improvement in DNNs' generalization performance, they focused on discovering neural networks' weaknesses. Firstly, Szegedy et al. showed that it is the entire space of activations rather than individual units that contains semantic information. The rest of their work is oriented in finding the DNN's blind spots. The most important findings made by Szegedy et al. in [11] are:

1. For all the networks studied, for every tested image, the authors were able to generate an adversarial example, which was for humans visually almost indistinguishable from original image, that was misclassified by the original network.
2. Cross model generalization: a large number of adversarial examples are misclassified by networks trained with different hyper-parameters (number of layers, initial weights, etc.).
3. Cross training-set generalization: a large number of examples are misclassified by networks trained on a disjoint training set.

These discoveries pose question related to how the universal approximators can be so vulnerable against such subtle changes. This discovery undermines smoothness property of neural networks claiming that inputs close to each other are supposed to be assigned to the same class. Their experimental results suggest that using adversarial examples in training process may improve generalization performance.

Moreover, Nguyen et al. [9] were experimenting with creating visually meaningless images, which were classified by a neural network as one of the image categories with high confidence reaching 99.99 %. The authors named these examples "fooling images". Nguyen et al. made a hypothesis that these fooling examples are caused by the discriminative nature of classifier, permitting the algorithm to find an example that is far away from discriminative boundary as well as from all the data that have been seen before.

Goodfellow et al. [3] were trying to discover the reason why adversarial examples exist. They claim, existence of adversarial examples stem from models being *too linear*. Authors believe, adversarial perturbations are dependent on model's weights, which are similar for different models learned to perform the same task. They observed, a generalization of adversarial noise across different natural examples is caused by the fact that adversarial perturbations are not dependent on a specific point in space but on direction of the perturbation. Further in the work by Goodfellow et al., experiments comparing resistance of models with different capacity against adversarial and fooling examples have been performed. In their paper it was shown that models, which are simple to optimize yield easily to adversarial and fooling examples, thus they have no capacity to resist these perturbations. Adversarial training is presented by Goodfellow et al. as a possible tool for further regularization (than solely use methods such as dropout).

Gu and Rigazio [4] used various pre-processing methods to diminish adversarial perturbations. They have tested several denoising procedures including: injection of additional Gaussian noise with subsequent Gaussian blurring, more sophisticated methods using autoencoder trained on adversarial examples, and a standard denoising autoencoder. Gu and Rigazio believe DNN's sensitivity is affected by training procedure and the objective function rather than by network topology. As a possible solution to achieve local generalization in the input space, they propose a deep contractive neural network.

The contribution of this work, in relation to the mentioned studies is in investigating the network sensitivity to adversarial noise affected by dropout regularization applied to various combinations of network layers. Apart from adversarial noise examination, robustness methods are inspected when dealing with random noise. Moreover, this research contains a study of adversarial noise resistance of committees and combinations of robustness methods. Human object recognition accuracy has been reported [1, 12] and compared to accuracy of DNNs examined on natural images. An open question is how the accuracy changes on noisy images. To answer this question, this paper presents a comparison of human visual recognition ability of images distorted by different types of noise, with the performance of the state of the art deep convolutional neural network.

3   Perturbations and Robustness Methods

This section introduce the different types of perturbations used in the experiments, along with well-known robustness methods and the proposed method.

3.1 Perturbations

To examine neural network robustness, various perturbations are designed to corrupt an image. A perturbed image $\tilde{X}$ is composed of original image X where each element is in range $(0,1)$ and additive noise R, expressed as $\tilde{X} = X + R$. In our framework, two noise types are used as an additive noise. Random noise taken from Gaussian distribution and non-random adversarial noise obtained by gradient sign method [3]:

$$R = \epsilon \, \text{sign}(\nabla_X L(\boldsymbol{\theta}, X, \mathbf{y})). \tag{1}$$

The adversarial noise is created by a model with parameters $\boldsymbol{\theta}$ for input data X with the corresponding target vector $\mathbf{y}$ via a sign function for the gradient of the loss function $L(\boldsymbol{\theta}, X, \mathbf{y})$.

3.2 Distortion Measure

To make a simple comparison of the amount of noise that is injected to images, a measure is designed, the average distortion per pixel $dist$ for the whole data set, independent of type of the noise:

$$dist = \frac{1}{n}\frac{1}{c}\frac{1}{h}\frac{1}{w} \sum_{k=1}^{n}\sum_{l=1}^{c}\sum_{i=1}^{h}\sum_{j=1}^{w} \left| \tilde{X}_{klij} - X_{klij} \right|. \tag{2}$$

Average noise is calculated over all color channels c, image height h and image width w for every picture in the set containing n elements.

This distortion measure facilitates a comparison of perturbed images at similar noise quantification levels. Images perturbed with Gaussian-generated noise and with gradient sign noise, which are the main concern of the article, are visually compared in Fig. 1.

3.3 Robustness Methods

To face problems caused by adversarial noise, several methods for increasing robustness of DNN's have been proposed. The following section start with description of well-known robustness methods and end by characterizing the proposed method for dealing with adversarial noise.

Dropout. Dropout is a regularization method presented by Hinton et al. [5], which prevent networks from overfitting by dropping out random nodes along with their connections in each training iteration. This method can be applied to one or more layers. For each layer, a different probability to skip a node may be used. In each training iteration, a different thinned network is trained. Output from all the thinned networks can be easily approximated by using the whole network with activations scaled by the probability of the node is used in the training phase. The method comes with a price of longer training time (two to three times as reported by Srivastava et al. [10]).

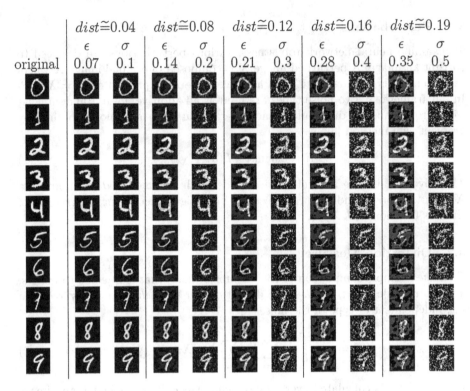

Fig. 1. Visualization of MNIST images affected by random and gradient sign noise at different distortion levels.

Low-Pass Filter. Low-pass filtering is an input pre-processing method, which uses blurring/denoising convolution to clean noise, see Gu and Rigazio [4]. To boost the blurring effect on adversarial noise, before applying the convolutional filter, regions created by adversarial noise are destroyed with additive Gaussian noise. This process aims to move input image from unrecognizable regions to the form in which it can be correctly classified.

Denoising Autoencoder. Denoising autoencoder (DAE) is a generative neural network that is used to reconstruct corrupted inputs. It was used by Gu and Rigazio [4] as a pre-processing method with purpose to clean input image of adversarial noise. This is facilitated by its symmetric bottleneck network topology.

Adversarial Training. A one way to increase robustness of a neural network is to train the network on its own adversarial examples. Szegedy et al. [11] tested a procedure, in which a neural network was trained on set regularly updated by a pool of newly created adversarial examples. Goodfellow et al. [3] used another approach, training a neural network on an ordinary training set using an adversarial objective function.

Adversarial Committee. It has been shown [11] that other models are less affected by adversarial examples than the model, which the examples are designed to perturb. Models trained on adversarial examples show good performance when classifying adversarial examples of another model. Based on these observations, we propose a committee of models trained on adversarial examples. A standard model, trained on natural training set is consecutively trained on its own adversarial examples. Adversarial examples used to train the model are created in two stages. In the first stage, gradient sign noise examples are created. The second stage involves addition of gradient scaled by a constant to the gradient sign noise examples. For many natural images, a magnitude of the gradient is too small compared to the range of input parameters. Gradient magnitude of an adversarial example greatly exceeds gradient magnitude of the natural image, hence we use the gradient sign noise images to produce the gradient instead of natural images. The training image

$$\tilde{X} = X + R + c\nabla_X L(\boldsymbol{\theta}, X + R, \mathbf{y})) \tag{3}$$

is produced as a linear combination of a gradient sign noise example $X + R$ (Eq. 1) and a gradient of the loss function for the gradient sign image scaled by a constant c. After a fixed amount of training iterations a snapshot of the model is saved and used to produce new examples that update training set pool. All of these snapshots including the model trained purely on natural training set are combined into a committee. In deployment stage, the committee outputs an average prediction of all committee members. An advantage of this method is that it is difficult to generate gradient sign noise for the committee, since its members are trained to recognize images corrupted with noise derived from other committee members.

4 Experimental Setup

The robustness is observed on MNIST data-set, for which the baseline is obtained from a modification of the original LeNet network [7], see Fig. 2. The network is initialised by Xavier algorithm [2], trained by stochastic gradient descent while using momentum and L2 regularization.

4.1 Robustness Experiments

We measure robustness in form of generalization error obtained for 100 test sets, all originated from MNIST test set, perturbed to have different distortion levels. Results from different test sets facilitate graphical visualization of how the error changes with increased distortion.

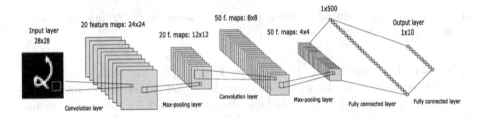

Fig. 2. Architecture of LeNet network, composed of two convolution layers, two max-pooling layers, and two fully connected layers.

Table 1. Layer-specific dropout rate (rate at which nodes are being randomly dropped out) of models used in experiments.

Abbreviation	Input	Conv1	Conv2	Full	Output	Train iterations
Inp	0.2	0	0	0	0	35000
All	0.2	0.2	0.2	0.5	0.5	40000

At first, a robustness of models with dropout applied to various layers is measured. Details (dropout rates) of models created by performing dropout on different layers of LeNet are contained in Table 1.

Further experimentation determines effect of low-pass filter and denoising autoencoder pre-processing on models' robustness. Low-pass filter is used to remove high frequencies representing the noise. For this purpose, three Gaussian convolution kernels of sizes 3×3, 5×5 and 7×7 were designed. Each kernel was filled with Gaussian function defined in range (-3, 3). Function's variance was chosen for each filter separately, under restriction that classification error on clean set cannot cross 1 %. Variances of 0.6, 1.3 and 7 were chosen for filters of size 7, 5 and 3 respectively. The effect of filtering applied to adversarial examples is enhanced by injecting Gaussian noise to images before the filter is applied.

Low-pass filter pre-processing is compared with pre-processing of denoising autoencoder (DAE). Experimental DAE with structure 784-1000-500-250-30-250-500-1000-784 is trained by Nesterov's accelerated gradient. Denoising effect is achieved by applying dropout on the input layer. Robustness to adversarial noise is facilitated by stacking fully trained denoising autoencoder to the bottom layer of LeNet. Denoising autoencoder cleans data from noise and feed clean images to LeNet's input layer. Three stacked networks have been created: denoising autoencoder stacked to LeNet and denoising autoencoder stacked to LeNet with dropout on input layer and to LeNet with dropout on input, conv1, conv2, full and output layer (Table 1).

Adversarial training in the proposed constellation is realized by training the model with its own adversarial examples. Networks trained on adversarial examples originate from LeNet model trained for 10000 iterations, regularized by weight decay. This model is further consecutively trained for 5 times, each time for 5000 iterations on current set of adversarial examples joined with training sets of previous models. After every phase of adversarial training a new model is created. All of these 6 models are combined to a committee. To point out their robustness, a comparison with basic committee composed of 6 models is demonstrated.

4.2   Human Noise Processing Experiments

In our experiments, the performance of human ability to recognise digits is obtained for four different sets of images that are presented to test subjects, three of them originating from MNIST test set and one from USPS [6] data set. One of the sets is composed of 15 natural images, the other two sets consists of natural images corrupted either by Gaussian noise or by gradient sign noise. Each noise type set contains 6 subsets per 15 images with graduating noise levels. Noise levels are designed to have similar distortions for pairs of Gaussian and gradient sign noise subsets. Gradient sign noise levels are defined by $\epsilon = 0.07, 0.14, 0.21, 0.28, 0.34, 0.4$ matched with Gaussian noise levels created using $\sigma = 0.09, 0.18, 0.27, 0.36, 0.45, 0.54$. The last set of 10 images are taken from USPS dataset and resized to match dimensions of MNIST pictures. Digits on these images are written in a way that may be difficult for humans to decipher, thus they are noted in this work as the "human adversarial noise".

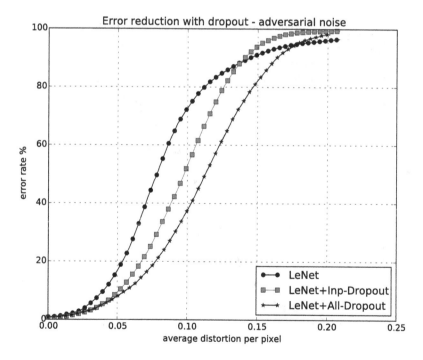

Fig. 3. Generalization error of models regularized with dropout on input layer (Inp-Dropout) and on all the layers (All-Dropout) compared to standard model when classifying adversarial examples.

Each mentioned noise level subset is randomly picked from the whole set of 10000 images, except for USPS images, of which 5 images per each digit are available and exactly one per digit is randomly chosen for the test. Subsets are shuffled and presented to test subject via a Python script, which captures subject's decisions and stores them for future analysis.

The data essential to carry out the experiment was gathered from 57 subjects. Every subject has classified a set of 205 images described in previous paragraphs. The accuracy is compared for each noise level separately. Each participant contributes with an average accuracy of his choices for each noise type and level separately. A collection of these accuracies achieved by all tested subjects is used to compute mean and standard deviation, which are compared with values obtained from tests of 20 LeNet models in the same experimental setup.

5   Results

5.1   Dropout

A two LeNet models (see Table 1) were trained with dropout regularization and tested for resistance to gradient sign adversarial noise. Regularizing network with dropout made the network more robust to adversarial distortion up to large

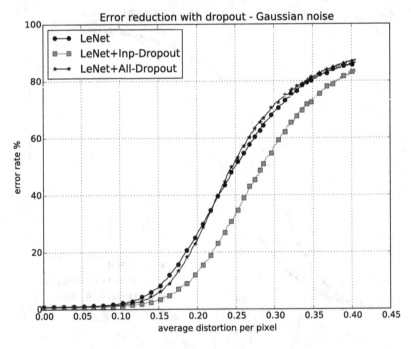

Fig. 4. Generalization error of models regularized with dropout on input layer (Inp-Dropout) and on all the layers (All-Dropout) compared to standard model when classifying images corrupted with Gaussian noise.

levels of distortion (> 0.15) where all models perform poorly. The most robust solution was obtained by applying dropout on every layer. Error on adversarial examples with $\epsilon = 0.2$ was reduced from basic model error of 78.88 % to 42.97 % (see Fig. 3).

The same models regularized with dropout were tested for robustness by gradually increasing levels of Gaussian noise. As Fig. 4 depicts, the most resistant model to random noise was a model regularized with dropout only in the input layer. Applying dropout to other layers seem to have negative effect on robustness to random noise.

5.2 Pre-processing Methods

In the experiments for pre-processing methods, images are processed either by low-pass filter or by denoising autoencoder. Pre-processed pictures were further fed into two different models to be classified, to an ordinary LeNet model and to a LeNet regularized with dropout. The denoising autoencoder has been found better at preparing adversarial examples for classification than low-pass filter. The highest accuracy has been achieved by pre-processing adversarial examples by a denoising autoencoder and subsequent classification by LeNet regularized by dropout on all the layers (see Fig. 5).

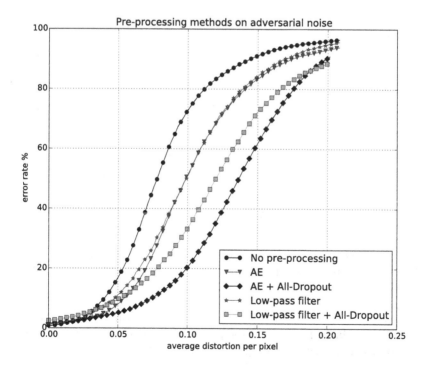

Fig. 5. Generalization error of LeNet when classifying pre-processed adversarial examples. Images are pre-processed either by low-pass filter or by denoising autoencoder.

Table 2. Generalization error (%) of robustness methods on MNIST test set perturbed at three different distortion levels.

Method	dist=0	dist=0.1	dist=0.2
No method	0.83	73.6	96.1
Dropout	0.91	35.7	98.1
Low-pass filter	1.38	52.0	95.0
DAE	1.27	52.4	93.2
Low-pass filter + dropout	2.51	34.8	88.5
DAE + dropout	1.56	21.4	90.3
Standard committee	0.86	70.9	97.2
Adversarial training after 5 stages	0.87	44.5	92.1
Committee of models trained on adv. examples	0.65	9.8	36.5

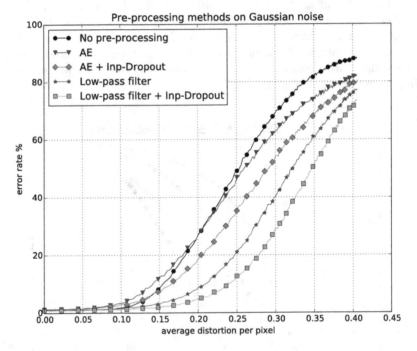

Fig. 6. Generalization error of LeNet when classifying preprocessed images corrupted by Gaussian noise. Images are preprocessed either by low-pass filter or by denoising autoencoder.

By examining the resistance of these methods to random noise, different results were obtained. Low-pass filter prepared randomly distorted images for classification better than denoising autoencoder. When dealing with Gaussian noise, encouraging results were achieved by low-pass filtering of images, later classified by LeNet regularized with dropout on the input layer (see Fig. 6).

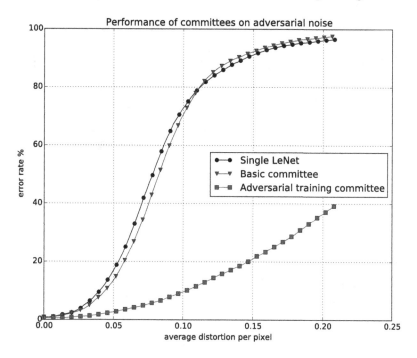

Fig. 7. Generalization error of committees on adversarial noise. Performance of committee trained on adversarial noise is compared to performance of a basic committee.

5.3   Adversarial Training and Committees

As has been shown before [3], a standard committee does not provide desired robustness. To demonstrate the resistance of a committee of models trained on adversarial examples we propose, robustness tests comparing generalization error of this committee with the error of a standard committee and a single model are conducted (see Fig. 7). A committee of 6 models trained on adversarial examples gave an error of 36.5 % on MNIST adversarial examples with $\epsilon = 0.37$ compared to error of a single model 96.1 % or to the error of a basic averaging committee with the same amount of members, 97.2 %. Table 2 compares results with other robustness methods.

5.4   Human Recognition Experiments

The performance is evaluated by calculating the accuracy as a ratio of correctly classified images to the total number of tested images. The results of human vision experiments are illustrated as curves composed of mean values for gradually increasing levels of each noise type separately, see Fig. 8. Curves are encapsulated by their 95 % confidence regions. The experiment indicates that humans classify images (corrupted by Gaussian noise) with similar accuracy as the deep neural networks. Experiment also suggests, humans find adversarial and random

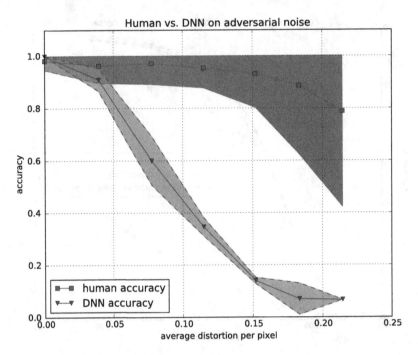

Fig. 8. Classification accuracy of humans compared to the accuracy of 20 LeNet models when classifying adversarial examples. Mean values are bounded by 95 % confidence regions. Plot depicts, the performance of LeNet on adversarial noise is far inferior to performance of humans.

noise similarly problematic. In contrary, DNNs suffer a significant decrease in classification performance when classifying adversarial examples, compared to human performance on adversarial examples (see Fig. 8) or to DNNs' performance on random noise.

6   Discussion and Conclusion

For the MNIST dataset, we exploited fast and simplistic method (the gradient sign method) of creating adversarial examples. Due to the small number of output classes, one color channel and low image resolution, adversarial examples on MNIST are notably different from original images, however, far more harmful than randomly distorted images. Thus robustness experiments might be more accurate on datasets such as CIFAR100 or ImageNet that contain many image classes.

Dropout experiments in this paper suggest, regularization by dropout on every network layer is more effective on adversarial examples than using dropout just on input layer. Adversarial noise is affecting every layer, through which the gradient has been backpropagated, making adversarial noise more dependent on model's internal structure. Using dropout on model internal structure complicates creation of new adversarial examples. Random noise is more likely compensated by learning from incomplete inputs than by dropping out nodes in every network layer. A possible reason to this lies in the fact that, random noise is independent of model structure. During training, model is learning to recognize incomplete patterns, becoming more robust to single pixel random deviations.

Moreover, a few observations while comparing input pre-processing methods deserved to be noted. Low-pass filtering prepares an image distorted by random noise for correct classification better than the denoising autoencoder. Gaussian low-pass filter is a simple and powerful tool to suppress random Gaussian noise by averaging. Our results suggest that, adversarial examples reconstructed by denoising autoencoder are easier for neural network to classify than adversarial examples blurred by a low-pass filter. A possible explanation may be that the gradient sign noise splits image into regions, which are moved by the noise in the same direction. Averaging filter that performs well on random noise has small or almost no effect within these regions, whereas autoencoder is not limited to simple averaging.

Also, models trained on adversarial examples are consistently more robust to adversarial noise created by other models. Average prediction of these models forming a committee diminishes the chance to perturb the committee by exploiting the weakest model. We come to conclude, an ensemble of models trained on adversarial noise is more resistant to adversarial noise than any single model we have tested so far, for the MNIST dataset.

This paper also reported human accuracy when classifying images corrupted by random and adversarial noise. From obtained results, we come to an assumption, humans classify images perturbed by adversarial and by random noise with similar accuracy, unlike DNNs. DNNs' performance suffers greatly when classifying adversarial examples. Accuracy has been measured on an inconsistent test set. To avoid overfitting to a small set of images, every test subject was presented with different subset of images. Hence input set variance may have biased the results. For future work, there is an opportunity for a similar experiment: testing each participant on the same image set, comparing the results to the results already obtained by this paper's experiments.

Acknowledgments. We would like to express our gratitude to all participants of the human visual recognition experiment.

References

1. Cireşan, D., Meier, U., Masci, J., Schmidhuber, J.: Multi-column deep neural network for traffic sign classification. Neural Netw. **32**, 333–338 (2012)
2. Glorot, X., Bengio, Y.: Understanding the difficulty of training deep feedforward neural networks. In: Proceedings of the International Conference on Artificial Intelligence and Statistics (AISTATS 2010). Society for Artificial Intelligence and Statistics (2010)

3. Goodfellow, I.J., Shlens, J., Szegedy, C.: Explaining and harnessing adversarial examples. CoRR abs/1412.6572 (2014). http://arxiv.org/abs/1412.6572
4. Gu, S., Rigazio, L.: Towards deep neural network architectures robust to adversarial examples. CoRR abs/1412.5068 (2014). http://arxiv.org/abs/1412.5068
5. Hinton, G.E., Srivastava, N., Krizhevsky, A., Sutskever, I., Salakhutdinov, R.: Improving neural networks by preventing co-adaptation of feature detectors. CoRR abs/1207.0580 (2012). http://arxiv.org/abs/1207.0580
6. Hull, J.J.: A database for handwritten text recognition research. IEEE Trans. Pattern Anal. Mach. Intell. **16**(5), 550–554 (1994)
7. Lecun, Y., Bottou, L., Bengio, Y., Haffner, P.: Gradient-based learning applied to document recognition. Proc. IEEE **86**(11), 2278–2324 (1998)
8. Lecun, Y., Cortes, C.: The MNIST database of handwritten digits. http://yann.lecun.com/exdb/mnist/
9. Nguyen, A., Yosinski, J., Clune, J.: Deep neural networks are easily fooled: high confidence predictions for unrecognizable images (2015)
10. Srivastava, N., Hinton, G., Krizhevsky, A., Sutskever, I., Salakhutdinov, R.: Dropout: a simple way to prevent neural networks from overfitting. J. Mach. Learn. Res. **15**, 1929–1958 (2014). http://jmlr.org/papers/v15/srivastava14a.html
11. Szegedy, C., Zaremba, W., Sutskever, I., Bruna, J., Erhan, D., Goodfellow, I.J., Fergus, R.: Intriguing properties of neural networks. CoRR abs/1312.6199 (2013). http://arxiv.org/abs/1312.6199
12. Taigman, Y., Yang, M., Ranzato, M., Wolf, L.: Deepface: closing the gap to human-level performance in face verification. In: 2014 IEEE Conference on Computer Vision and Pattern Recognition (CVPR), pp. 1701–1708, June 2014

Predicting the RCGA Performance
for the University Course Timetabling Problem

Noel Rodriguez-Maya[1]([✉]), Juan J. Flores[2], and Mario Graff[3]

[1] Instituto Tecnolgico de Zitacuaro, Ex Hacienda de Manzanillos SN,
Zitacuaro, Michoacan, Mexico
`nrodriguez@itzitacuaro.edu.mx`
[2] Universidad Michoacana de San Nicolas de Hidalgo,
Av. Fco. J. Mugica SN, Morelia, Michoacan, Mexico
`juanf@umich.mx`
[3] INFOTEC - Centro de Investigacion e Innovacion en Tecnologias de la Informacion
y Comunicacion, Catedras CONACyT, Ciudad, Aguascalientes, Mexico
`mario.graff@infotec.com.mx`

Abstract. The University Course Timetabling Problem (UCTP) is a
well known optimization problem. Literature reports different methods
and techniques to solve it, being Evolutionary Algorithms (EA) one of the
most successful. In the EA field, the selection of the best algorithm and
its parameters to solve a particular problem, is a difficult problem; would
be helpful to know a priori the performance related to that algorithm.
Fitness Landscape Analysis (FLA) is a set of tools to describe optimization problems and for the prediction of the performance related with EA.
FLA uses a set of metrics to characterize the landscape depicted by a
cost function, aiming to understand the behaviour of search algorithms.
This work presents an empirical study to characterize some instances
of UCTP, and for the prediction of difficulty exhibited by Real-Coded
Genetic Algorithms (RCGA) to solve the instances. We used FLA as
characterization schema; neutrality, ruggedness, and negative slope coefficient are the metrics used in the analysis. To test and validate the
proposal, we use three UCTP instances based on Mexican universities.
Incipient results suggest an correlation between the negative slope coefficient and the difficulty exhibited by RCGA in the solution of UCTP
instances. Ruggedness and neutrality provide the global structure of the
instances's landscape.

Keywords: Optimization · Fitness Landscape Analysis · Genetic
Algorithms · University Course Timetabling Problem

1   Introduction

The University Course Timetabling Problem (UCTP) is a combinatorial problem whose general objective is to find the best combination of resources covering
certain needs and satisfying a set of constraints. Resources are represented by

A. Martin-Gonzalez and V. Uc-Cetina (Eds.): ISICS 2016, CCIS 597, pp. 31–45, 2016.
DOI: 10.1007/978-3-319-30447-2_3

lecturers, classrooms, and time slots, among others, and needs, generally, are the academic courses offered by the university. Constraints are grouped in two: *hard constraints* are restrictions that cannot be violated, and *soft constraints*, are desirable to maintain, but are not absolutely critical. Given its complexity, literature reports different approaches to solve these kind of problems. Evolutionary Algorithms (EA) is one of the most widely used tools to solve UCTP.

When EA users face these problems, they usually face two types of problems: what is the best EA to solve the problem?, and what are the best parameter settings for the algorithm? To select the best solver, it is necessary to establish a picture about the problem. That is, a deepest study about the structure and difficulty of the problem can give us some insights about the expected performance. The results of the study can also provide insight about the best parameter settings for the solver.

In the field of EA, one of the most successful techniques to try to understand the topology and dynamics of optimization problems, is Fitness Landscape Analysis (FLA). FLA uses a set of Fitness Landscape (FL) metrics to try to describe the problem and give some indications about its difficulty. Those metrics measure different FL features, e.g.: the rate of ruggedness, neutrality, deceptiveness, gene interaction, evolvability, etc.

In this work we use Real-Coded Genetic Algorithms (RCGA) as the problem solver. RCGA uses the same heuristic, and genetic operators than its binary version. RCGA has been used for solving different kinds of optimization problems; it has been able to solve the majority of them. For the characterization of UCTP instances and a possible prediction of performance of RCGA, we perform an empirical FLA on a set of three UCTP instances. Then, we related the overall performance obtained by RCGA in the solution of the UCTP instances with the results obtained by the FL metrics. To perform the FLA, we use some of the most representative landscape features to measure the global structure of problems and the metaheuristic's evolvability. We use ruggedness and neutrality to measure the global structure of problems and negative slope coefficient to measure the evolvability of the metaheuristic. Those metrics characterize the problem and try to determine the difficulty of the algorithm for solving the problems. These metrics can be described as follows.

- *Ruggedness* is related to the multimodal properties of landscapes. In a rugged FL the individuals of many EA can get trapped in local optima as a consequence of premature convergence [8].
- *Neutrality* is related to the presence of regions with similar fitness values, called neutral areas. Neutral Networks (NN) [6] are interconected points in the search space with similar fitnesses. [2,3,11].
- *Negative Slope Coefficient* is related to the level of evolvability of neighbours. To measure evolvability, NSC uses the concept of Fitness Cloud (FC) [19]. FC uses the fitnesses of the individuals against fitnesses of its neighbors to create a set of clouds. For each cloud, the fitness mean is calculated, and these values serve as points to set a slope; this slope measures the problem's difficulty.

FLA is applied to three Mexican universities: Instituto Tecnologico de Zitacuaro, Instituto Tecnologico del Valle de Morelia, and Instituto Tecnologico de Tuxtla Gutierrez. The information about the study cases (lecturers, classrooms, time slots, etc.) was collected from those universities as close to reality as we could. The main contributions of this work are: (1) the use of a set of FL metrics applied to a real-coded metaheuristic, (2) the study of a set of UCTP instances based on Mexican universities, and (3) the empirical characterization of UCTP instances to try to relate with the performance exhibited by RCGA. Results suggest some correlation between the FL features and the performance exhibited by RCGA, negative slope coefficient obtained the highest correlation with the difficulty of problems, ruggedness and neutrality obtained indications about global structure of problems's landscapes.

This paper is organized as follows: Sect. 2 presents the related work, Sect. 3 describes the main concepts about Fitness Landscape Analysis, Sect. 4 presents the problem statement and formulation of the University Course Timetabling Problem, Sect. 5 presents details about experimentation and the main results, Sect. 6 presents a brief discussion, and and Sect. 7 presents conclusions and further research directions.

2   Related Work

The main aim of FLA is understanding the topology of optimization problems, it establishes an approximate scenario where an algorithm performs the search, and by means of FLA we can predict the behaviour of algorithms [12].

Many works are based on Fitness Landscape Coefficient (FDC); the main purpose of FDC is the determination of the deceptiveness of optimization problems: the more deceptive landscape, the harder the problem. For using FDC is necessary to know the global optimal (or some optimal solution) to perform a correlation between a set of fitness and a set of distances to such optimal value. In [14] authors use FDC to measure the search difficulty of a specific sample from some online instances (www.metaheuristic.net); their results show a correlation between fitnesses and distances which is a good indication the difficulty of problems. In [15] the authors propose the use of evolvability indicators to try to capture the evolvability of EA; they use FDC and Negative Slope Coefficient (NSC) as indicators. Results show good estimation of difficulty for Genetic Programming problems.

Ventresca [18] et al. predict the hardness of some instances of the vehicle routing problem which is considered as a combinatorial NP-hard problem (similar to UCTP. To predict the hardness, they use Information Content which measures the ruggedness with respect to the flat or neutral areas of the landscape. To test its approach, they use a total of 66 problems, and different genetic operators using GA as optimization method; their results are grouped into clusters and they are correlated with its quality solution.

Ochoa et al. [10] propose an schema based on hyper-heuristic (heuristic to find heuristics), on a timetabling scenario, their purpose is to find the best low-level heuristic to solve the UCTP. They propose to analyze that scenario using a fitness landscape analysis, they uses the fitness distance correlation and auto-correlation analysis tools. Their results are based on the qualitative properties of the analyzed landscape.

Other approaches use a set of intrinsic metrics (e.g. skewness, kurtosis, among others) to make learning models: Kostuch [4] et al. use a linear model to predict the hardness of EA when solving the UCTP; the predictors are based on intrinsic UCTP properties, their results suggest a strong correlation between the intrinsic properties of UCTP instances and the performance of EA to solve them.

3 Fitness Landscape Analysis

We can define Fitness Landscape as the tuple $\mathcal{L} = (\mathcal{S}, f, \mathcal{N})$, where $\mathcal{S}$ is the search space of feasible solutions, $f : \mathcal{S} \to \mathbb{R}$ is a fitness function, and $\mathcal{N}(\cdot)$, is the neighbourhood function [18] that assigns to every $s \in \mathcal{S}$ a set of neighbour solutions defined in Eq. 1.

$$\mathcal{N}(s, \delta) = \{\forall s' \in \mathcal{S} | s \neq s' \wedge d_E(s, s') \leq \delta\} \tag{1}$$

where δ is the maximum euclidean distance between s and its neighbours. There are many methods to calculate the neighbour for a solution, in some cases neighbour is defined as that solution that can be reached through the application of a single genetic operator, or a solution that is localized at certain distance (generally, euclidean distance).

Fitness Landscape Analysis (FLA) uses a set of FL metrics to try to understand the intrinsic properties of optimization problems. Some metrics are specialized to measure certain structural properties of problems (such as neutrality and ruggedness) while other are specialized to measure the level of evolvability (negative slope coefficient) of the metaheuristics. The following paragraphs define the FL metrics used in this work.

3.1 Neutrality

In the field of EA, neutral regions are areas of the FL that have similar fitness values [6], i.e. similar fitness values within a neighbourhood. Neutrality is the rate of neutral areas in $\mathcal{S}$, Eq. 2 computes an estimate of neutrality based on a sample $\mathcal{S}$.

$$\text{neutrality}(\delta, \gamma) = \frac{\sum_{s \in \mathcal{S}} \frac{|\mathcal{N}\mathcal{N}(s, \delta, \gamma)|}{|\mathcal{N}(s, \delta)|}}{|\mathcal{S}|} \tag{2}$$

where $\mathcal{S}$ is a set of points from the search space, δ is the maximum distance between neighbours, and γ is the maximum distance between two fitnesses considered as similar, $\mathcal{N}\mathcal{N}(\cdot)$ is the neutral neighborhood function defined in Eq. 3, and $\mathcal{N}(\cdot)$ is the neighbourhood function defined in Eq. 1.

$$\mathcal{N}\mathcal{N}(s, \delta, \gamma) = \{\forall s' \in \mathcal{S} | s \neq s' \wedge d_E(s, s') \leq \delta \wedge d_E(f(s), f(s')) \leq \gamma\} \tag{3}$$

High rates of neutrality, are not desirable in an FL to produce an evolutive environment [13], i.e. neutrality can affect the distribution of local optima and as a consequence the success of searching [8].

3.2 Ruggedness

There are many techniques to measure the level of ruggedness [7,17]; in particular, this work uses entropy to measure it [7]. Entropy measures ruggedness by means of three-point paths. A 3-point path is: neutral when the points have equal fitnesses, smooth when the fitnesses of points change in one direction, and rugged when the fitnesses of points change in two directions [7].

A sequence of fitness values $S = \{\phi_t\}_{t=1}^n$ is formed by a set of points selected from a random walk sampling [7]. The sequence is represented by a string $S(\gamma) = s_1 s_2 s_3 ... s_n$ of symbols $s_i \in \{\bar{1}, 0, 1\}$ obtained by Eq. (4). The parameter γ is a real number that determines the accuracy of the calculation of $S(\gamma)$; the lower the value of γ, the more sensitive the difference between neighbouring fitness values will be.

$$s_i = \Psi_{\phi_t}(i, \gamma) = \begin{cases} \bar{1}, & \text{if } \phi_i - \phi_{i-1} < -\gamma \\ 0, & \text{if } |\phi_i - \phi_{i-1}| \leq \gamma \\ 1, & \text{if } \phi_i - \phi_{i-1} > \gamma \end{cases} \quad (4)$$

Equation (5) measures the level of entropy $H(S)$ exhibited by the sequence S.

$$H(S) = -\sum_{p \neq q} P_{[pq]} log_6 P_{[pq]} \quad (5)$$

where p and q are elements from the set $\{\bar{1}, 0, 1\}$, and number 6 (in the log function), represents all possible shapes of the sequence. $H(S) \in [0, 1]$ is a rate of the variety of shapes present in the Fitness Landscape, which only considers the subset of rugged elements. The higher the value of $H(S)$, the wider the variety of rugged shapes in S [7]. $P_{[pq]}$ is calculated according to Eq. 6:

$$P_{[pq]} = \frac{n_{[pq]}}{n} \quad (6)$$

where $n_{[pq]}$ is the number of sub-blocks pq in the sequence $S(\gamma)$. For each rugged element, $P_{[pq]}$ calculates the probability of occurrance of that element.

3.3 Negative Slope Coefficient

Let f be a fitness function that assigns a real value to each individual x, and $V(x_j) = \{v_1^j, v_2^j, ..., v_n^j\}$ the set of neighbours of a given individual $x_j, \forall j \in [1, n]$. The neighbours are obtained by applying one step of a genetic operator. To sample the neighbours, the k-tournament selection algorithm was used (using 10 individuals in the tournament). Fitness Cloud (FC) is a 2-dimensions plot where abscissas are the set of all individuals's fitnesses, and the ordinates the fitnesses of their neighbours, see Eq. (7).

$$FC = \{(f(x_j), f(v_k^j)), \forall j \in [1, m], \forall k \in [1, n]\} \quad (7)$$

once the FC is determined, each element of abscissas and ordinates are split into k segments $\{I_1, I_2, ..., I_k\}$, $\{J_1, J_2, ..., J_k\}$, $\forall k \in [1, m]$. The averages of abscissa

$\{M_1, M_2, ..., M_k\}$ and ordinates, $\{N_1, N_2, ..., N_k\}$, $\forall k \in [1, m]$ are calculated. The segment set $S = \{S_1, S_2, ..., S_{k-1}\}$, where each S_i connects the points (M_i, N_i) to point (M_{i+1}, N_{i+1}) is created. The slope set P is calculated, where $P_i = (N_{i+1} - N_i)/(M_{i+1} - M_i)$, $\forall i \in [1, k-1]$. The Negative Slope Coefficient is computed by the Eq. 8.

$$nsc = \sum_{i=1}^{k-1} min(0, P_i) \qquad (8)$$

Based on nsc, Vanneschi et al. [16] proposed the following hypothesis to classify problems: If $nsc = 0$ the problem is easy, if the $nsc < 0$ then the problem is difficult and the value of nsc quantifies this difficulty: the smaller its value, the more difficult the problem is.

4   University Course Timetabling Problem

The University Course Timetabling Problem (UCTP) consists of fixing a sequence of meetings between lecturers, classrooms, and time slots to a set courses, satisfying different constraints. Each course, lecturer, classroom, and time slot has special features and specifications. The UCTP is defined as an optimization problem where the aim is to minimize the number of constraints violations, which was set as the performance value: the fewer constraints violated the better the timetable's performance.

4.1   Problem Statement

The UCTP can be defined as follows. Given the following preliminary definitions: $\mathbb{C}$ is a set of courses $c_i \in \mathbb{C}$, $i \in [1, N_\mathbb{C}]$, $\mathbb{L}$ is a set of lecturers $l_j \in \mathbb{L}$, $j \in [1, N_\mathbb{L}]$, $\mathbb{R}$ is set of classrooms $r_k \in \mathbb{R}$, $k \in [1, N_\mathbb{R}]$, $\mathbb{T}_1$ is a set of available times in the week (from monday to thursday) $a_l \in \mathbb{T}_1$, $l \in [1, N_{\mathbb{T}_1}]$, $\mathbb{T}_2$ is a set of available times on friday $b_m \in \mathbb{T}_2$, $[m \in 0, 1, ..., N_{\mathbb{T}_2}]$. All the indices start at 1, except the index for $\mathbb{T}_2$ which starts at 0, to simplify the cases when a course does not occur in a given day (i.e., if does not have an assigned time).

The constraints are represented by the following functions:

- $\mathcal{H}(\cdot)$ is a function that returns the penalization for the hard constraints, constraints are: (1) a classroom cannot be assigned to more than one course in the same time/day, or a lecturer cannot be assigned to more than one course in the same time/day, (2) the number of weekly hours assigned to a course must match the course's needs.
- $\mathcal{S}(\cdot)$ is a function that returns the penalization for the soft constraints, constraints are: (1) classrooms must be assigned consecutively (no holes in schedule), (2) check the suitable classroom (theory or practice), (3) chek if teacher not pass his/her assignment hours (4) the lecturer profile must match the course requirement, (5) the assigned classrooms must satisfy the needs of course capacity, and (6) check the preference of lecturers's time,

The objective is to minimize the penalization of hard constraints ($\mathcal{H}$) and soft constraints ($\mathcal{S}$); the hard constraints must be fulfilled and the soft constraints must be minimized [1]. A mathematical formulation can be represented by:

Determine an assignment $[X_{l,r,t_1,t_2}]_{N_C}$ that minimizes [5]:

$$f(X) = \sum_{i=1}^{2} \mathcal{H}(X) + \sum_{j=1}^{6} \mathcal{S}(X) \tag{9}$$

Subject to:

$$x \in [a, b] \tag{10}$$

$$\forall j \in [1, N_L], \forall k \in [1, N_R], \forall l \in [1, N_{T_1}],$$
$$\forall m \in [1, N_{T_2}], \sum_{c \in C} \mathcal{S}(x_{j,k,l,m}) \geq 0 \tag{11}$$

$$\forall j \in [1, N_L], \forall k \in [1, N_R], \forall l \in [1, N_{T_1}],$$
$$\forall m \in [1, N_{T_2}], \sum_{c \in C} \mathcal{H}(x_{j,k,l,m}) = 0 \tag{12}$$

$f(X)$ computes the total penalization for a given X Eqs. (9) and (10) checks the interval values for each dimension, the soft constraints can be violated Eqs. (11) and (12) prevents hard constraint violations.

4.2 Solution Based on Genetic Algorithms

Our approach uses a real-coded Genetic Algorithms (RCGA) chromosome representation, which allows us to solve the problem directly. The chromosome is a vector of real values, where each gene represents a possible combination of resources (lecturer, classroom, and time slots) assigned to a task (a course).

$$C = [l_i, r_i, t_{1i}, t_{2i}], i \in [1, N_C] \tag{13}$$

where $l \in [1, \ldots, N_L]$, $r \in [1, \ldots, N_R]$, $t_1 \in [1, \ldots, 12]$, and $t_2 \in [0, \ldots, 12]$ are the different genes to be mutated. Algorithm 1 shows the RCGA based solution for the UCTP.

Algorithm 1. *RCGAsolution* ($\mathbb{C}$, $\mathbb{L}$, $\mathbb{R}$, $\mathbb{T}_1$, $\mathbb{T}_2$)

1: $\Omega \leftarrow \mathbb{L} \times \mathbb{R} \times \mathbb{T}_1 \times \mathbb{T}_2$
2: i = 0;
3: *initialize* P(i, Ω);
4: *evaluate* P(i, $\mathbb{C}$);
5: **while** i $\leq$ *number-of-generations* **do**
6:     i = i + 1;
7:     *select* P(i) *from* P(i-1);
8:     *recombine* P(i);
9:     *evaluate* P(i, $\mathbb{C}$);
10: **end while**
11: return $[best\_individual_{l,r,t_1,t_2}]_{N_C}$

The sets $\mathbb{C}$, $\mathbb{L}$, $\mathbb{R}$, $\mathbb{T}_1$, $\mathbb{T}_2$ (courses, lecturers, classrooms, times 1 and times 2 respectively) are passed as parameters to the algorithm, the search space Ω is created (line 1), from Ω at time i, the initial population P is generated (line 3), each individual from P is evaluated according to Eq. (9) (line 4). Once the initialization process ends, the iterative process is started while the number of generations is not reached (line 5). Time is increased (line 6). The selection of individuals from population P at time i is performed (line 7), the mutation-crossover processes is performed on the population P at time i (line 8), the evaluation of population P at time i is performed (line 9). Finally the $[best\_individual_{l,r,t_1,t_2}]_{N_C}$ (solution) is returned.

4.3 Study Cases

The complexity of academic schedules is due to the resources to be assigned to a set of courses, and the courses's specific characteristics. The following paragraphs describe the instances considered in this work.

Instituto Tecnologico de Zitacuaro (ITZ) is a public university located at the east of state of Michoacan, Mexico. ITZ offers 8 academic programs, the total needs to be covered in each period (semester) for the 8 academic programs is a total of 181 courses offered in each period.

Instituto Tecnologico del Valle de Morelia (ITVM) is a public university located at the center of state of Michoacan, Mexico. ITVM offers 5 academic programs, the total needs to be covered in each period (semester) for the 5 academic programs is a total of 112 courses offered in each period.

Instituto Tecnologico de Tuxtla Gutierrez (ITTG) is a public university located at the state of Chiapas, Mexico. ITTG offers 8 academic programs, the total needs to be covered in each period (semester), for the 8 academic programs is a total of 180 courses offered in each period.

Table 1 shows the sets of tasks and resources available for each university.

Table 1. Tasks and resources available for each UCTP instance.

Task	ITZ	ITVM	ITTG
Courses ($\mathbb{C}$)	181	112	180
Lecturers ($\mathbb{L}$)	69	122	218
Classrooms ($\mathbb{R}$)	34	38	102
Available times per week, from monday to thursday ($\mathbb{T}_1$)	12	12	12
Available times on friday ($\mathbb{T}_2$)	12	12	12

Table 1 shows the quantitative characteristics of the studied UCTP instances, however, to perform an optimization process and as consequence a fitness landscape analysis, it is necessary to know details about resources and needs. The following list shows the qualitative information used for each resource/need.

- **Courses:** name, academic program, its group, number of hours (theory and practical), ideal profile(s). Each course is assigned to a group. Each group has the following specifications: semester and academic program.
- **Lecturers:** name, department, profiles (having 3 profiles as maximum), number of available hours, and preferred schedule.
- **Classrooms:** label, type (theory or practice), and its capacity.
- **Time 1:** is the time slot to be assigned between Monday to Thursday, using time slots of two hours.
- **Time 2:** is the time slot to be assigned on Friday, using time slots of one hours.

5 Experiments and Results

This section presents the main results of this work: first we show the parameter setting used by both the RCGA and the FL metrics, and finally, we show the results obtained by the Fitness Landscape Analysis.

5.1 Parameter Settings

Table 2 shows the parameter setting used by the RCGA.

Table 2. RCGA parameter settings.

Parameter	Value
Population size	500
Number of generations	1000
Crossover type	Arithmetical
Crossover rate	70 %
Mutation rate	30 %
Selection	Tournament of size 10
Codification	Real

We define performance as the rate of successful trials where the global optimum was found in GA experiments; we set the number of trials to 100 and the maximum number of generations to 1,000.

To perform the FLA, for each UCTP instance, we sampled the search space using a uniform random distribution (in the case of neutrality and NSC) and a random walk sequence (in the case of ruggedness) with 1000 points. Table 3 show the parameters used by the FL metrics.

where f^{max} and f^* are the maximum and minimum fitness values, respectively, L_u and U_b are the lower and upper bounds of the search space defined by the fitness function (see Eq. 9). Experiments were repeated 100 times and the mean was reported.

Table 3. Parameters of Fitness Landscape metrics.

FL metric	Parameter-value
Neutrality	$\delta = d_E(L_b, U_b) \times 0.1, \gamma = |f^{max} - f^*| \times 0.1$
Ruggedness	$\gamma = |f^{max} - f^*| \times 0.1$
Negative slope coefficient	evolvability = one step of genetic operators

5.2 Results of Fitness Landscape Analysis

The following figures show some landscape features depicted by the UCTP instances: (1) Figs. 1, 2 and 3 show a picture of the ruggedness depicted by the instances; the search space was sampled using 100 points in random walk, and its fitness was plotted, (2) Fig. 4 shows fitness values obtained from the instances; we select the best 100 fitness values from a total of 10000 (from a random uniform distribution), then, we plot those fitnesses in order.

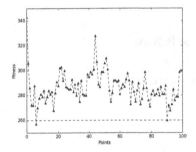

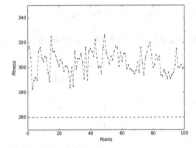

Fig. 1. Ruggedness in the ITZ instance.   **Fig. 2.** Ruggedness in the ITVM instance.

Figures 1, 2 and 3 give us some indications about the ruggedness for the instances: all the instances presented high rates of ruggedness. Figure 4 shows the ordered fitness distribution for all the instances: the ITTG instance has the worst fitness values (the highest values), the ITZ instance presents the best, and the ITVM instance has the second worst fitness distribution. To establish a numerical description, the following Tables 4 and 5 show the rates of ruggedness for the UCTP instances.

In Table 4 the ITVM and ITTG instances have the highest rates of ruggedness, while the ITVZ instance had the lowest rate. These measures confirm the rugged landscape depicted by the instances's fitness function; all the instances presented high rates of ruggedness.

Table 5 shows similar rates of neutrality for all the instances; in all the instances, approximately 35 % of landscapes presents neutral regions, that is, regions where the fitness is similar between neighbours. These measures give us general indications about the landscape where the search is performed: in general

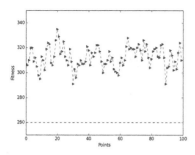

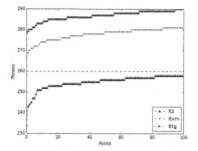

Fig. 3. Ruggedness in the ITTG instance.

Fig. 4. Ordered fitnesses for the UCTP instances.

Table 4. Rates of ruggedness in the UCTP instances.

	Ruggedness			
Instance	min	max	μ	σ
ITZ	0.55	0.83	0.75	0.060
ITVM	0.78	0.85	0.82	0.015
ITTG	0.70	0.85	0.79	0.025

terms the search is performed in rugged landscapes with low rates of neutrality. In literature we can find that, generally, for the GA, the more rugged landscape, the more difficult problem [9]. However, coupled with the descripcion of the landscape, it is necessary to perform an analysis about the algorithm's features, to get the difficulties presented by the algorithm in the solution of problems. To get an algorithmic point of view (level of improvements for the GA), we measure the GA's evolutionary level with the negative slope coefficient. Table 6 shows the NSC value for all the instances.

The ITTG instance obtained the lowest value, the ITVM the highest value, and the ITZ the second lowest value. According with Vanneschi et al. [16], the more negative value, the more difficult problem. In this case the ITTG instances would be the harder problem followed by the ITZ instance.

Table 5. Rates of neutrality in the UCTP instances.

	Neutrality			
Instance	min	max	μ	σ
ITZ	0.293	0.413	0.356	0.027
ITVM	0.299	0.453	0.363	0.034
ITTG	0.300	0.491	0.373	0.033

Table 6. Evolvability of GA using negative slope coefficient.

University	min	max	μ	σ
ITZ	−1.60	0.0	−0.54	0.339
ITVM	−1.02	0.0	−0.37	0.205
ITTG	−2.03	0.0	**−0.77**	0.438

A direct comparison between the difficulty presented in GA (through NSC) against the overall performance of GA for the UCTP instances, would not be fair, because the distribution of fitness values are no the same for the instances (as we can see in Fig. 4). To set a fairer scenario about the prediction of performance for the GA, we can compare the performance exhibited by the GA with the level of performance improvements using different number of generations in the GA. Figure 5 shows the overall performance using different number of generations $\{100, 200, 300, 400, 500, 600, 700, 800, 900, 1000\}$, and Fig. 6 shows the final performance using 1000 generations for all the UCTP instances.

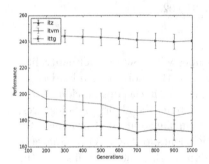

Fig. 5. Generations vs GA performance.

Fig. 6. Final GA performance for all the UCTP instances.

According to Fig. 5 we can establish the following facts:

- ITZ, initial performance 182.86, final performance 171.4, obataining a final improvement of 6 %.
- ITVM, initial performance 204.2, final performance 185.9, obataining a final improvement of 9 %.
- ITTG, initial performance 247.3, final performance 240.53, obataining a final improvement of 3 %.

If we evaluate the level of improvement, the most difficult problem is the ITTG instance, the ITVM instance is the easiest, and the ITZ instance is in the middle. These results are correlated with the levels of difficulty presented in Table 6. Another important characteristic is the final performance obtained on those problem instances. We can see in Fig. 6 how the performance obtained by the ITZ and ITVM instances are similar despite the difference of its fitness distribution (Fig. 4): the level of improvement for the ITVM instance is better than the ITZ instance, then the ITVM instance should be the easiest instance.

6   Discussion

Nowadays, the prediction of the performance of Evolutionary Algorithms has received attention by researchers around the world. The possible solution could give new tools to solve problems, that is, the user will be focused on the problem not on the algorithms and their parameter settings. Despite University Course Timetabling is a well known optimization problem, commonly solved by EA, there are only a few works focusing on its characterization. Perhaps, the main obstacle to characterize these problems is the sustancial difference between instances.

To characterize, and predict the performance of UCTP instances, we propose the use of fitness landscape analysis (FLA). To perform the FLA we use some of the most successful fitness landscape metrics: ruggedness, neutrality, and negative slope coefficient. To perform the optimization process we used the real-coded version of Genetic Algorithms (Real-Coded Genetic Algorithms). To test and validate our proposal we use three different UCTP instances, the instances are based on real-life Mexican universities.

Ruggedness and neutrality give us indications about the features of the landscape; ruggedness give us the fitness landscape distribution while neutrality give indications about neutral areas into the landscapes. In this empirical study, according to literature, the hardest instance (the ITTG instance) was not correlated with the more rugged landscape, perhaps because the landscapes have similar rates of ruggedness and neutrality.

The negative slope coefficient give us indications of evolvability in the GA process, according to Vanneschi et al. [16] the lower its value, the harder the problem. The ITTG instances obtained the worst level of evolvability, while the ITVM instance obtained the best evolvability, contrary to the final performance values obtained by the GA process, where ITTG and ITZ obtained the worst and best performances (Fig. 6), respectively. On the other hand, if we measure the level of performance improvement varying the number of generations (Fig. 5), and the fitness distribution for each instance (Fig. 4) against its performance (Fig. 6), we can see relation between negative slope coefficient and its related performance. The ITTG instance is the most difficult instance, the ITVM instance is the easiest instance, and the ITZ is in the middle, this has a direct relation with the difficulty obtained by negative slope coefficient (Table 6).

7   Conclusions and Further Research

This contribution presents an empirical study of fitness landscape analysis on the University Course Timetabling Problem, using Real-Coded Genetic Algorithms as optimization solver. To test and validate this work, we use three Mexican universities with different features, we performed a fitness landscape analysis on those universities and compared the performance exhibited by GA against the measures. We use as landscape metrics: ruggedness, neutrality and negative slope coefficient. Results suggest a correlation between the negative slope coefficient and the difficulty exhibited by the RCGA to solve the instances. In our future work we will focus on the use of more UCTP instances, we will incorporate other fitness landscape measures, and the use of other Evolutionary Algorithms.

References

1. Abdullah, S., Turabieh, H., McCollum, B., McMullan, P.: A hybrid metaheuristic approach to the university course timetabling problem. J. Heuristics **18**(1), 1–23 (2012)
2. Harvey, I., Thompson, A.: Through the labyrinth evolution finds a way: a silicon ridge. In: Higuchi, T. (ed.) Proceedings of the First International Conference on Evolvable Systems: From Biology to Hardware (ICES 1996), pp. 406–422 (1996)
3. Katada, Y., Ohkura, K., Ueda, K.: Measuring neutrality of fitness landscapes based on the nei's standard genetic distance. In: Proceedings of 2003 Asia Pacific Symposium on Intelligentand Evolutionary Systems: Technology and Applications, pp. 107–114 (2003)
4. Kostuch, P., Socha, K.: Hardness prediction for the university course timetabling problem. In: Gottlieb, J., Raidl, G.R. (eds.) EvoCOP 2004. LNCS, vol. 3004, pp. 135–144. Springer, Heidelberg (2004)
5. Lara, C., Flores, J.J., Calderón, F.: Solving a school timetabling problem using a bee algorithm. In: Gelbukh, A., Morales, E.F. (eds.) MICAI 2008. LNCS (LNAI), vol. 5317, pp. 664–674. Springer, Heidelberg (2008)
6. Galván-López, E., Poli, R.: Some steps towards understanding how neutrality affects evolutionary search. In: Runarsson, T.P., Beyer, H.-G., Burke, E.K., Merelo-Guervós, J.J., Whitley, L.D., Yao, X. (eds.) PPSN 2006. LNCS, vol. 4193, pp. 778–787. Springer, Heidelberg (2006)
7. Malan, K., Engelbrecht, A.P.: Quantifying ruggedness of continuous landscapes using entropy. In: IEEE Congress on Evolutionary Computation, pp. 1440–1447. IEEE (2009)
8. Malan, K.M., Engelbrecht, A.P.: A survey of techniques for characterising fitness landscapes and some possible ways forward. Inf. Sci. **241**, 148–163 (2013)
9. Marn, J.: How landscape ruggedness influences the performance of real-coded algorithms: a comparative study. Soft Comput. **16**(4), 683–698 (2012)
10. Ochoa, G., Qu, R., Burke, E.K.: Analyzing the landscape of a graph based hyperheuristic for timetabling problems. In: Proceedings of the 11th Annual Conference on Genetic and Evolutionary Computation, GECCO 2009, pp. 341–348. ACM, New York (2009)
11. Poli, R., López, E.G.: The effects of constant and bit-wise neutrality on problem hardness, fitness distance correlation and phenotypic mutation rates. IEEE Trans. Evol. Comput. **16**(2), 279–300 (2012)
12. Shiau, D.-F.: A hybrid particle swarm optimization for a university course scheduling problem with flexible preferences. Expert Syst. Appl. **38**(1), 235–248 (2011)

13. Smith, T., Philippides, A., Husbands, P., O'Shea, M.: Neutrality and ruggedness in robot landscapes. In: Proceedings of the 2002 Congress on Evolutionary Computation, CEC 2002, vol. 2, pp. 1348–1353 (2002)
14. Sultan, A.B.M., Mahmod, R., Sulaiman, M.N., Bakar, M.R.A., Abdullah, M.T.: Fitness distance correlation (FDC) as a hardness prediction for university course timetabling problem. Jurnal Teknologi **49**(1), 87–92 (2012)
15. Trujillo, L., Martínez, Y., Galván López, E., Legrand, P.: A comparative study of an evolvability indicator and a predictor of expected performance for genetic programming. In: Proceedings of the Fourteenth International Conference on Genetic and Evolutionary Computation Conference Companion, GECCO Companion 2012, pp. 1489–1490. ACM, New York (2012)
16. Vanneschi, L., Tomassini, M., Collard, P., Vérel, S.: Negative slope coefficient: a measure to characterize genetic programming fitness landscapes. In: Collet, P., Tomassini, M., Ebner, M., Gustafson, S., Ekárt, A. (eds.) EuroGP 2006. LNCS, vol. 3905, pp. 178–189. Springer, Heidelberg (2006)
17. Vassilev, V.K., Miller, J.F., Fogarty, T.C.: Digital circuit evolution and fitness landscapes. In: Angeline, P.J., Michalewicz, Z., Schoenauer, M., Yao, X., Zalzala, A. (eds.) Proceedings of the Congress on Evolutionary Computation, vol. 2, pp. 6–9. IEEE Press, Mayflower Hotel, Washington (1999)
18. Ventresca, M., Ombuki-Berman, B., Runka, A.: Predicting genetic algorithm performance on the vehicle routing problem using information theoretic landscape measures. In: Middendorf, M., Blum, C. (eds.) EvoCOP 2013. LNCS, vol. 7832, pp. 214–225. Springer, Heidelberg (2013)
19. Verel, S., Collard, P., Clergue, M.: Where are bottlenecks in nk fitness landscapes? CoRR, abs/0707.0641 (2007)

Photovoltaic Module Temperature Estimation: A Comparison Between Artificial Neural Networks and Adaptive Neuro Fuzzy Inference Systems Models

J. Tziu Dzib[1], E.J. Alejos Moo[1], A. Bassam[1(✉)], Manuel Flota-Bañuelos[1],
M.A. Escalante Soberanis[1,2], Luis J. Ricalde[1], and Manuel J. López-Sánchez[1]

[1] Facultad de Ingeniería, Universidad Autónoma de Yucatán,
Av. Industrias no contaminantes, Mérida, Yucatán, Mexico
josetziu@me.com, e.alejos@outlook.com, mauricio.escalante@hotmail.com,
{baali,manuel.flota,lricalde,manuel.lopez}@correo.uady.mx
[2] Clean Energy Research Centre, University of British Columbia, 2360 East Mall,
Vancouver, BC V6T 1Z3, Canada

Abstract. The main objective of this paper is to present a comparison between two models for estimation of a photovoltaic system's module temperature (T_{mod}) using Artificial Neural Networks and Adaptive Neuro Fuzzy Inference Systems. Both estimations use measurements of common operation variables: current, voltage and duty cycle (d) from a power converter of the photovoltaic system as input variables and T_{mod} as a desired output. The models used the same database for the training process, different training strategies were evaluated with the objective to find which model has the best estimation with respect to the T_{mod}. Subsequently, the output results from these architectures are validated via the Root Mean Squared Error, Mean Absolute Percentage Error and correlation coefficient. Results show that the Artificial Neural Network model in comparison with Adaptive Neuro Fuzzy Inference System model provides a better estimation of T_{mod} with $R = 0.8167$. Developed models may have an application with smart sensors on cooling systems for photovoltaic modules with the objective of improving their operation efficiency.

Keywords: Renewable energy · Artificial intelligence · Photovoltaic system · Module temperature · Levenberg-Marquardt algorithm · Statistical comparison

1 Introduction

The energy of Sun is the most abundant energy source on planet earth, it is renewable and available for direct or indirect use, i.e. solar radiation, wind, biomass, thermal, etc. If only 0.1 % of the solar energy that reaches the earth could be turned into electrical energy at an efficiency of 10 %, there would be 4 times

© Springer International Publishing Switzerland 2016
A. Martin-Gonzalez and V. Uc-Cetina (Eds.): ISICS 2016, CCIS 597, pp. 46–60, 2016.
DOI: 10.1007/978-3-319-30447-2_4

more energy available than the world production capacity (5000 GW) [1]. One way to harvest this energy source is through the use of photovoltaic (PV) technology. Over the last decade, PV technology has had a rapid increase in usage compared to other types of renewable energy sources [2]. A Photovoltaic module (PVM) converts solar radiation into Direct Current (DC) which is transferred to a power condition unit [2], this means that high levels of radiation improve the overall output of the PVM, but this has a side effect. Higher levels of radiation mean that the flux of photons moving within a PV cell is also higher, which results in an increase in temperature of the PVM [3]. However, the rise in temperature within the module reduces its efficiency, thus producing low levels of voltage and current [4], this causes a problem since it is necessary to extract as much energy as possible from the system in order to make it effective. The implementation of cooling systems offers a solution to this problem, but these systems require exact measurements of T_{mod} for their optimal operation [5]. However, temperature sensors are usually imprecise, require maintenance and are sensible to climate conditions such as ambient temperature, wind speed, radiation flux and thermal properties of the materials of the PVM, making them unreliable when used on these systems [6]. Estimation methods offer an alternative to temperature sensors, although, the unpredictability and the non-linear behavior of the temperature tends to be a problem when trying to estimate it. Artificial Intelligence (AI) techniques have recently had multiple applications on engineering in general and this is due to the fact that they provide a better solution as these often do not need statistic data and solve problems more complex than their own programming at higher speeds [7]. AI covers multiple techniques such as Artificial Neural Networks (ANN), Adaptive Neuro Fuzzy Inference Systems (ANFIS), amongst others.

Different publications related to application of ANN and ANFIS on PV technology can be found elsewhere. García-Domingo et al. [8] proposed an electric characterization of a concentrating PV using ANN. Paul et al. [9] presented an ANN model to identify and optimize statistics representing insulation availability by a solar PV system. Mellit et al. [10] estimated the power produced of a photovoltaic module with an ANN estimation model. Salah and Ouali [11] proposed two methods of maximum power point tracking using ANN and ANFIS controllers for PV systems. Salaiman [2] presented the modeling of operating PV module temperature using ANN with solar irradiance and ambient temperature as inputs for the ANN architecture.

The aim of this investigation is to design ANN and ANFIS models to estimate the T_{mod} of a PV system and compare these two models to determinate which is the best for estimation of this variable. This paper is organized as follows: an overview on PV experimental systems is proposed in the second section, artificial neural networks and adaptive neuro fuzzy inference system models are described in the third section, the fourth section is devoted to the training, results and comparison process. Finally, conclusions are presented.

2   Material and Method

2.1   Photovoltaic Experimental System

A photovoltaic setup was developed and installed in order to acquire experimental data and evaluate its performance, the PV system was installed in Mérida, Yucatán, México (20°56'18.2"N 89°36'55.8" W), a schematic diagram of this setup is illustrated in Fig. 1. The system consists of a solar PVM, a current sensor with a 0 to 20/40/80 ADC selector and 0–5 VDC output, a voltage sensor, a miniature infrared temperature sensor, a data acquisition (DAQ) USB Device, and finally, a laptop with NI *LabView*™ software, see Table 1 for component models.

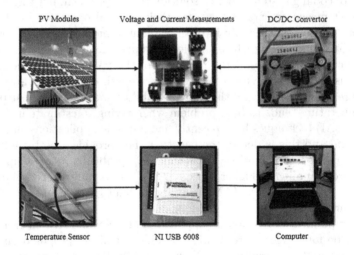

Fig. 1. Schematic diagram for experimental system setup.

The measured T_{mod} was taken by the infrared temperature sensor, the voltage and current of the PVM were measured with the voltage and current sensors, respectively with a duty cycle d set by the DC/DC converter. Finally, this data is collected in a synchronized pattern using the DAQ USB Device and then dispatched to the computer where it is analyzed via *LabView*™, this software provides a user-friendly interface and allows the setting of sampling time intervals.

The database consists of registers taken every 10 s, at 20 min an average value of the registers is calculated in order to obtain a representative sample and the result is moved into the database. Sample consisting of a total of 1045 data pairs with significant temperature variations (see Fig. 5) was selected for training and validation purposes of the AI models, this sample presents PVM parameters under different climate conditions. Table 2 illustrates a list of input and output variables used for the ANN and ANFIS models; Figs. 2, 3 and 4 represent

Table 1. Photovoltaic experimental systems characteristics.

Component	Model
Photovoltaic module	YL110Wp
Current sensor	H970LCA
Voltage sensor	MCR-VDC-UI-B-DC
Temperature sensor	PM-HA-21-MT-CB
DAQ device	NI USB-6008/6009
Laptop	1.8 GHz i7 8DB DDR3 RAM

graphical behavior of Current (I), Voltage (V) and Duty Cycle (d) respectively as input variables, and Fig. 5 represent the behavior of module temperature as output variable.

Table 2. Characteristics of input and output variables about ANN and ANFIS models.

Parameters	Samples	Min.	Max.	Unit
Input				
d	1045	20	60	-
Voltage	1045	0.0048	33.2325	V
Current	1045	4.8428e-04	3.3232	A
Output				
Temperature	1045	289.6500	312.5389	K

2.2 Artificial Neural Network

ANN is an interconnected set of processing units that uses mathematical and computational techniques to solve problems from complicated, imprecise or missing data [12]. Each of these units is called a perceptron or neuron and has an incoming weight, bias and an output given by the transfer function of the sum of the inputs, see Fig. 6. The function of the output neuron can be mathematically expressed as:

$$u(x, w) = \sum_{i=1}^{n} f(w_i x_i + b), \qquad (1)$$

where $u(x, w)$ is the output of the neuron, w_i is the synaptic weights, x_i is the input data and b is the bias value.

An ANN is generally organized on three layers: Input, hidden and output layer [13]. The ANN training can be divided in two phases: The first phase consists of updating the neuron activation values with a chosen learning algorithm,

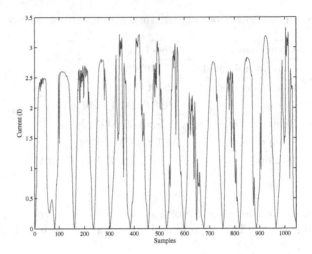

Fig. 2. Graphical representation of the current.

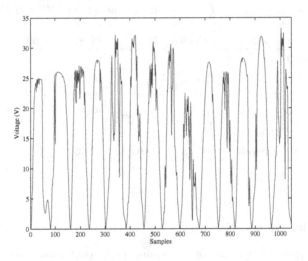

Fig. 3. Graphical representation of the voltage.

the second phase updates weights to minimize the function error measuring the difference between the desired and actual output [14].

Developing an ANN requires selection of the optimal training architecture, often set using information given by the experience and knowledge of the user [2].

2.3   Adaptive Neuro Fuzzy Inference System

ANFIS is a multilayer network that uses neural network learning algorithms and fuzzy logic to map an input space to an output space. There are two types of fuzzy inference systems (FIS): Mamdani [15] and Sugeno [16]; Mamdani being more

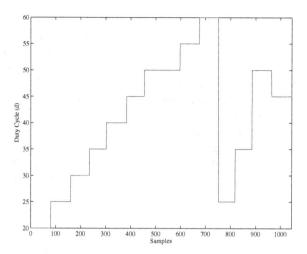

Fig. 4. Graphical representation of the duty cycle.

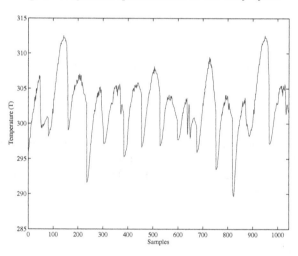

Fig. 5. Graphical representation of the module temperature.

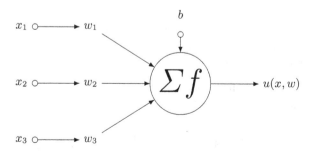

Fig. 6. A typical elementary network with 3 inputs.

intuitive and suited to human input, whereas Sugeno is more computationally efficient and works well with optimization and adaptive techniques. The consequence parameter in Sugeno FIS can be either a linear equation or a constant coefficient. The linear equation called "first-order Sugeno FIS" and the constant coefficient called "zero-order Sugeno FIS" are proposed by Jang [18]. Given the advantages of the Sugeno FIS, this model is used in this study, see Fig. 7.

Five layers are used to construct this system. Each layer consists of n number of nodes described by their function. Nodes denoted by squares are called "adaptive nodes", these represent parameter sets that are modifiable; nodes denoted by circles are called "fixed nodes", these fixed parameters set in the system. The output data from the nodes in a layer will be the input data of the next layer.

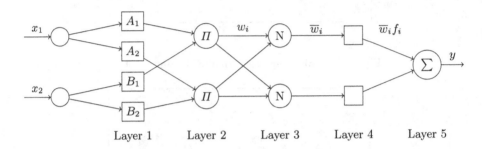

Fig. 7. Simplified ANFIS architecture.

To demonstrate the procedure of the ANFIS, a simple architecture is proposed. The system in Fig. 7 consists of two inputs, x_1 and x_2, and one output, y. Suppose the system is a first-order Sugeno FIS with a rule base contaning two fuzzy if-then rules expressed as:

Rule 1:
If x_1 is A_1 and x_2 is B_1,
then $f_1 = p_1 x_1 + q_1 x_2 + r_1$.
Rule 2:
If x_1 is A_2 and x_2 is B_2,
then $f_2 = p_2 x_1 + q_2 x_2 + r_2$.

where p_i, q_i and r_i $(i = 1, 2)$ are the linear parameters of the consequent part of the Sugeno FIS. Each layer of the model is as follows (note that O_i^j denotes the output of the i-th node and the j-th layer):

Layer 1: Input nodes. Each node in this layer generates membership grades for each input. For instance, the function of the i-th may be a Gaussian MF:

$$O_i^1 = \mu A_i(x) = e^{\frac{-(x_i - b_i)^2}{2a_i^2}}, i = 1, 2. \tag{2}$$

where x is the input to node i, A_i is the MF associated with this node and a_i, b_i are the parameters set that change the shape of the MF. Parameters in this layer are called *premise parameters*.

Layer 2: Rule nodes. Each node in this layer calculates the firing strength (output) of a rule via multiplication.

$$O_i^2 = w_i = \mu A_i(x_1)\mu B_i(x_2), i = 1, 2. \tag{3}$$

In ANFIS the total number of rules is given by Eq. (4)

$$R_n = j^i, \tag{4}$$

where i is the number of inputs, and j is the number of MFs per input.

Layer 3: Average nodes. Each node in this layer calculates the ratio of the i-th rule's firing strength to the total of all firing strengths:

$$O_i^3 = \overline{w}_i = \frac{w_i}{\sum_i w_i}, i = 1, 2. \tag{5}$$

Layer 4: Consequent nodes. Each node in this layer computes the contribution the i-th rule towards the overall output with the function:

$$O_i^4 = \overline{w}_i f_i = \overline{w}_i(p_i x_1 + q_i x_2 + r_i), i = 1, 2. \tag{6}$$

where $\overline{w}_i$ is the output of the layer 3, and p_i, q_i, r_i are the parameter sets. Parameters in this layer are called *consequent parameters*.

Layer 5: Output node. The single node in this layer computes the overall output as the sum of all contribution from each rule:

$$O_i^5 = y_1 = \sum_i \overline{w}_i f_i = \frac{\sum_i w_i f_i}{\sum_i w_i} \tag{7}$$

2.4   Statistical Criteria

For training, validation and comparison processes for ANN and ANFIS models, a statistical analysis is performed and applied using the following statistical test parameters: Correlation Coefficient (R), Root Mean Square Error (RMSE) and Mean Absolute Percentage Error (MAPE), see Table 3. R provides information on the linear relationship between the measured and estimated values. RMSE parameter is a frequently-used measure of the differences between values predicted by a model and the actual values observed. MAPE parameter is the absolute computed average of errors (%) by which estimated predictions of a variable differ from their actual values. The knowledge of this statistical parameter aids to evaluate whether the estimated predictions are underestimated or overestimated with respect to actual or expected data [19].

Where T_{mod} is the measured temperature and T_{sim} is the simulated temperature.

Table 3. Statistical criteria used for evaluation.

Statistical parameters	Equation
Correlation Coefficient (R)	$R = \dfrac{\sum_{i=1}^{N}(T_{mod}-\overline{T_{mod}})(T_{sim}-\overline{T_{sim}})}{\sqrt{\sum_{i=1}^{N}(T_{mod}-\overline{T_{mod}})^2(T_{sim}-\overline{T_{sim}})^2}}$
Root Mean Square Error (RMSE)	$RMSE = \sqrt{\frac{1}{N}\sum_{i=1}^{N}(T_{mod}-T_{sim})^2}$
Mean Absolute Percentage Error (MAPE)	$MAPE = \frac{1}{N}\sum_{i=1}^{N}\left|\frac{T_{mod}-T_{sim}}{T_{mod}}\right|$

3   Results and Discussion

3.1   Artificial Neural Network

Measurements of voltage and current from the PVM and the d factor from the DC/DC converter were selected as input variables for the ANN architecture, and T_{mod} of the PVM as the desired output. The number of neurons and transfer functions in the hidden layer must be adjusted to minimize the differences between the target and simulated output. $MatLab^{\mathrm{TM}}$'s neural network tool was used to train and estimate the measured data, with a total of 1045 data pairs used in this model, 80 % for training and 20 % for testing and validation. All results reached for the ANN architecture were trained with 1000 iterations of 1000 epochs.

The process to determine the learning algorithm, number of neurons in the hidden layer, and activation functions is frequently set using heuristic method. In this work, eight back-propagation algorithms were studied to determine the best

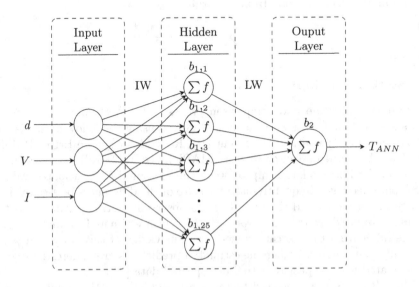

Fig. 8. Optimal ANN architecture reached.

Table 4. Comparison of back-propagation algorithms.

Back-propagation Algorithm	Mean Time (s)	RMSE	MAPE	R	Best linear equation
Levenberg-Marquardt	**2.21**	**2.4368**	**0.6413**	**0.8167**	**y = 0.67x + 99**
Bayesian regularization	19.12	2.4471	0.7753	0.8120	y = 0.62x + 91
Powell Beagle c. g.[a]	4.05	2.4827	0.8027	0.7801	y = 0.58x + 97
Batch gradient descent	13.16	2.6660	0.8851	0.6979	y = 0.58x + 108
One step secant	3.42	2.4418	0.8800	0.7969	y = 0.59x + 95
Batch gradient descent [b]	0.5	34.1916	8.6642	0.5049	y = 3.97x + 913
PolakRibiere [a]	2.44	3.1280	0.8014	0.6607	y = 0.44x + 169
Scaled [a]	1.00	3.1172	0.7930	0.6637	y = 0.44x + 168

[a] Conjugent gradient. [b] With momentum

T_{mod} estimation. Table 4 shows different back-propagation algorithms trained with 25 neurons in the hidden layer. Results show that the performance between Levenberg-Marquardt (RMSE = 2.4368) and Bayesian regularization (RMSE = 2.4471) algorithms are similar but differ in the mean time of convergence (2.21 and 19.12 s respectively), Levenberg-Marquardt was over eleven times faster than the Bayesian regularization. The best prediction was found with the Levenberg-Marquardt algorithm, this algorithm performs at RMSE=2.4368 with better linear fitting ($y = 0.67x + 99$) and an execution time of 2.21 s, this is due to the LM algorithm being designed to approach second order training speed without having to compute the Hessian matrix [20].

In order to find the most efficient transfer function, two different pairs of the transfer functions (Tansig-Purelin and Logsig-Purelin) were tested for the hidden and output layer respectively, varying the number of neurons in the hidden layer and training with LM algorithm. Logsig-Purelin were the functions with the best performance. A structure 3–25-1 presents a smaller RMSE (2.4368) and greater R (0.8167) than the values trained with a combination of Tansig-Purelin transfer function.

The optimum ANN architecture was found using an evaluation with different combinations of neurons. Table 5 illustrates the statistical comparison for different ANN architectures, the finest calculation is achieved by the ANN model with 25 neurons in the hidden layer, see Fig. 8. According to the results obtained about the RMSE, MAPE and R; values for training and testing are 2.4368, 0.6413 and 0.8167, respectively.

3.2 Adaptive Neuro Fuzzy Inference System

The ANFIS model (see Fig. 9) used in this study has three inputs (V, I, d), with five membership functions assigned to each input variable, which results in having 125 total rules according to Eq. (4). The input database (containing 1045 data

Table 5. Tests with different ANN architectures.

ANN architecture	No. neurons	RMSE	MAPE	R	Best linear equation
3-01-1	1	2.4934	0.7205	0.6364	y = 0.38x + 121
3-05-1	5	2.4890	0.6586	0.7835	y = 0.58x + 96
3-10-1	10	2.4925	0.6438	0.8100	y = 0.62x + 91
3-15-1	15	2.6713	0.6430	0.8131	y = 0.62x + 90
3-20-1	20	2.4514	0.6422	0.8149	y = 0.64x + 90
3-25-1	**25**	**2.4368**	**0.6413**	**0.8167**	**y = 0.67x + 99**
3-30-1	30	2.4494	0.6436	0.8153	y = 0.64 × 90

pairs) was randomly divided into learning and testing (80 % and 20 % respectively), obtaining good representation of the data distribution and to improve the overall training process. Several MF types were tested, including triangular, trapezoidal, generalized bell, Gaussian, sigmoidal and Pi; with 100 epoch in each training session using a hybrid learning algorithm, which uses a combination of the least-squares and back-propagation gradient descent methods to model a training data set [17]. Optimum parameters were found when checking data reached minimum RMSE.

Table 6. ANFIS performance with different types of membership functions.

Function	#MF	RMSE	MAPE	R	Best linear equation
Trimf	5	3.1623	0.7679	0.6574	y = 0.49x + 153
Trapmf	5	3.2504	0.7934	0.6345	y = 0.47x + 159
Gbellmf	5	3.1821	0.7866	0.6532	y = 0.49x + 153
Gaussmf	**5**	**2.5235**	**0.6566**	**0.7996**	**y = 0.64x + 108**
Gauss2mf	5	3.1258	0.7763	0.6634	y = 0.48x + 157
Pimf	5	3.4040	0.8013	0.6132	y = 0.50x + 150
Dsigmf	5	3.1239	0.7763	0.6638	y = 0.48x + 156
Psigmf	5	3.1239	0.7763	0.6638	y = 0.48x + 156

Table 6 illustrates the ANFIS performance with different types of MF, it can be observed that the best architecture was obtained with the FIS composed by Gaussian membership function with smaller RMSE = 2.5235, MAPE = 0.6566 and higher R = 0.7996.

3.3   Comparison of ANN and ANFIS Models

The estimation capability of the ANN and ANFIS models were individually evaluated by a linear regression analysis ($y = a + bx$) between the estimated

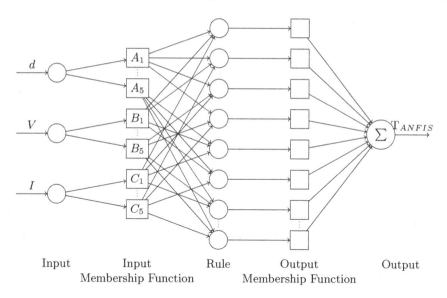

Fig. 9. ANFIS architecture used in this study. Input to Layer 3 connections are not shown.

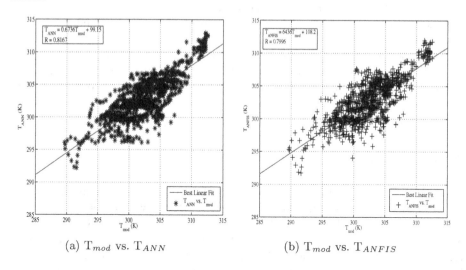

(a) T_{mod} vs. T_{ANN} (b) T_{mod} vs. T_{ANFIS}

Fig. 10. Comparison between error of the T_{mod}, ANN and ANFIS outputs respectively.

(T_{ANN} and T_{ANFIS} for ANN and ANFIS respectively) and measured (T_{mod}) data (using the correlation coefficient: R; the intercept: a; and the slope: b) under the same conditions [21]. Results obtained for ANN and ANFIS models are graphically shown in Fig. 10 (a, b).

The best linear regression equation for the ANN model was given by statistical parameters: a = 0.67 and b = 99 with R = 0.8120; whereas for ANFIS:

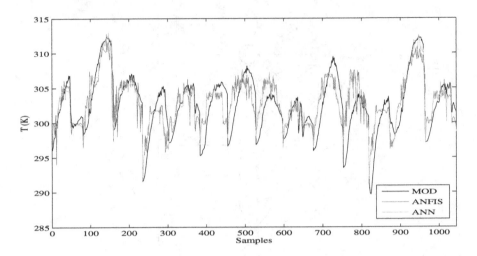

Fig. 11. Comparison between measured temperatures, ANN and ANFIS outputs.

a = 0.64 and b = 108 with R = 0.7996. According to these statistical analysis the ANN model estimation proved to be better than ANFIS for the T_{mod} approximation, although, the difference between ANN and ANFIS models is not outstanding.

With the purpose to illustrate the behavior of the estimated T_{mod} of the ANN and ANFIS in comparison with the measured data, Fig. 11 presents samples of ANN and ANFIS models estimations of this variable. It can be observed that ANN and ANFIS following the periodic behavior of the T_{mod} with ANN having better precision than ANFIS.

4   Conclusion

Application and comparison of ANN and ANFIS models for estimation of photovoltaic module temperature were investigated. Models with different functions were designed and trained by ANN and ANFIS methods. Values R, RMSE and MAPE were obtained for the ANN and ANFIS models. Comparing the performance of both models, the ANN model with Levenberg-Marquardt function had better performance in photovoltaic module temperature estimation and was selected as the best fitting model. It is also important to recognize that the prediction capability of the ANN and ANFIS could be significantly improved by an appropriate training with a larger number of field measurements under such conditions and the complex behavior of the module temperature. ANN and ANFIS could constitute useful and practical tools for the implementation of smart sensors that estimate the module temperature on a photovoltaic system. One of the applications of these smart sensors focuses in the employment of cooling systems to improve the operation performance of photovoltaic modules and increase their efficiency.

References

1. World Energy Council (WEC): Survey of Energy Resources 2013. WEC London (2013)
2. Sulaiman, S.I., Shah Alam, N.Z., Zainol, Z. Othman: Cuckoo search for determining Artificial Neural Network training parameters in modeling operating photovoltaic module temperature. In: Modelling, Identification & Control (ICMIC), pp. 306–309 (2014)
3. Butay, D.F., Miller, M.T.: Maximum peak power tracker: a solar application. Worcester Polytechnic Institute (2008)
4. Skoplaki, E., Palyvos, J.A.: On the temperature dependence of photovoltaic module electrical performance: a review of efficiency/power correlations. Sol. Energy **83**, 614–624 (2009)
5. Sherkar, G., Akkewar, A.: The cooling system of photovoltaic module and their effective efficiency. Int. J. Adv. Technol. Eng. Sci. **03**, 483–492 (2015)
6. King, D.L., Kratochvil, J.A., Boyson, W.E.: Temperature coefficients for PV modules and arrays: measurement methods. difficulties and results. In: Proceedings of the 26th IEEE Photovoltaics Specialists Conference, Anaheim, CA, USA, pp. 1183–1186 (1997)
7. Mellit, A., Benghanem, M.: Artificial neural network model for prediction solar ra-diation data: application for sizing stand-alone photovoltaic power system. In: Power Engineering Society General Meeting, Vol. 1, pp. 40–44 (2005)
8. García-Domingo, B., Piliougine, M., Elizondo, D., Aguilera, J.: CPV module electric characterisation by artificial neural networks. Renew. Energy **78**, 173–181 (2015)
9. Paul, D., Mandal, S.N., Mukherjee, D., Chaudhuri, S.R.B.: Artificial neural network modeling for efficient photovoltaic system design. In: Advanced Computer Theory and Engineering, pp. 50–56 (2008)
10. Mellit, A., Saglam, S., Kalogirou, S.: Artificial neural network-based model for estimating the produced power of a photovoltaic module. Renew. Energy **60**, 71–78 (2013)
11. Salah, C.B., Ouali, M.: Comparison of fuzzy logic and neural network in maximum power point tracker for PV systems. Electr. Power Syst. Res. **81**, 43–50 (2011)
12. Di Vi, M.C., Infield, D.: Artificial neural network for real time modelling of photovoltaic system under partial shading. In: Sustainable Energy Technologies, pp. 1–5 (2010)
13. Hasan, H., Bal, H.: Comparing performances of backpropagation and genetic algorithms in the data classification. Expert Syst. Appl. **38**, 3703–3709 (2011)
14. Malluhi, Q.M., Bayoumi, M.A., Rao, T.R.N.: An application-specific array architecture for feedforward with backpropagation ANNs. In: Application-Specific Array Processors, pp. 333–344 (1993)
15. Mamdani, E.H., Assilian, S.: An experiment in linguistic synthesis with a fuzzy logic controller. Int. J. Man-Mach. Stud. **7**(1), 1–13 (1975)
16. Sugeno, M.: Industrial Applications of Fuzzy Control. Elsevier Science Pub. Co., Amsterdam (1985)
17. Jang, J.S.R.: Fuzzy modeling using generalized neural networks and kalman filter algorithm. In: Proceedings of the Ninth National Conference on Artificial Intelligence (AAAI 1991), pp. 762–767 (1991)
18. Jang, J.S.R., Sun, C.T., Mizutani, E.: Neuro-Fuzzy and Soft Computing, p. 607. Prentice Hall, New York (1997)

19. Bassam, A., Álvarez del Castillo, A., García-Valladares, O., Santoyo, E.: Determination of pressure drops in flowing geothermal wells by using artificial neural networks and wellbore simulation tools. Appl. Thermal Eng. **75**, 1217–1228 (2015)
20. Hagan, M.T., Menhaj, M.B.: Training feedforward networks with the marquardt algorithm. IEEE Trans. Neural Netw. **5**, 989–993 (1994)
21. Vieira, J., Dias, F.M., Mota, A.: Artificial neural networks and neuro-fuzzy systems for modelling and controlling real systems: a comparative study. Eng. Appl. Artif. Intell. **17**, 265–273 (2004)

Thermal Efficiency Prediction of a Solar Low Enthalpy Steam Generating Plant Employing Artificial Neural Networks

O. May Tzuc, A. Bassam$^{(\boxtimes)}$, Manuel Flota-Bañuelos, E.E. Ordoñez López, Lifter Ricalde-Cab, R. Quijano, and Alan E. Vega Pasos

Faculty of Engineering, Autonomous University of Yucatan (UADY),
Av. Industrias no contaminantes por Periférico Norte, Apdo. Postal 150 Cordemex, Mérida, Mexico
maytzuc@gmail.com, {baali,mbolanos,eduardo.ordonez,oricalde, renan.quijano,alan.vega}@correo.uady.mx

Abstract. The present paper describes a mathematical model based on application of Artificial Neural Networks (ANN) employing a Multi-Layer Perceptron (MLP) model for thermal efficiency prediction of a solar low enthalpy steam generation plant composed by a Parabolic Trough Collector (PTCs) array. The MLP model uses physical data measurement in the steam prssoduction for heat processes. The input parameters used to achieve the prediction of thermal efficiency where: inlet and outlet working fluid temperature, flow working fluid, ambient temperature, direct solar radiation and wind velocity. After several training, the best MLP architecture was obtained employing Levenberg-Marquardt optimization algorithm, the logarithmic sigmoid transfer-function and the linear transfer-function for the hidden and output layer; and four neurons at the hidden layer, which predicts the thermal efficiency with a satisfactory determination coefficient ($R^2 = 0.99996$). The predictive model can be implemented at intelligent sensors that allow to improve control of the PTCs system and leads to better utilization of the solar resource.

Keywords: Photothermal systems · Parabolic trough solar collector · Mathematical model · Artificial intelligences

1 Introduction

In the last decades the rapid increase of energy demand has become a topic of vital importance. Of the total world-wide demand, more than 50 % of the energy is required for industrial processes, principally for heat processes generation [1]. However, almost all the global energy produced for heat processes is generated from fossil fuels, which causes several environmental impacts like global warming and climate change. These reasons show the need to replace the conventional energy generation for alternative and sustainable energy sources.

© Springer International Publishing Switzerland 2016
A. Martin-Gonzalez and V. Uc-Cetina (Eds.): ISICS 2016, CCIS 597, pp. 61–73, 2016.
DOI: 10.1007/978-3-319-30447-2_5

Among various renewable energies, solar energy is one of the best renewable sources for industrial applications because it is abundant, clean, cheap, free and present minimum environmental impact [2]. At the industry, there are several processes that require temperatures between the range of 80C and 250C; industries such as dairies, plastics, paper, canned food, textiles and among others, required thermal energy for processes like drying, sterilizing, cleaning, evaporation, steam and conditioning warehouses space for heating and cooling. This energy could be provided by photothermal solar collectors, specifically Parabolic Trough Solar Collectors (PTCs) [3,4]. Nevertheless, like all renewable energy systems, PTCs are linked to several variables and exposed to diverse fluctuations by the site climate condition, making the study of this systems very complex and consequently difficult to optimize its performance and to obtain the best cost-benefit at the operation process [5,6].

During the last years, the development of empiric models employing computational artificial intelligences techniques, like Artificial Neuronal Networks (ANN), has been shown as a powerful tool for complex problem solution from noisy and fluctuant data that cannot be solved using conventional methods; the same characteristics are present at most of renewable energy systems, reason for that this computing techniques have been adopted at the present for the modelling of renewable energies [7,8]. At the area of photothermal energy some examples of the use of ANN can be found in works like those made by Kaloguirou et al., [9] who developed an ANN model to predict the useful energy extracted from solar domestic hot water system, using has input data the physical characteristics of the system as collector area, storage type, mean storage tank heat loss, capacity, mean ambient temperature, mean cold water temperature and weather conditions. For the other hand, Géczy-Vg and Farkas [10] used data measurement from a domestic hot water system to develop a model by ANN to describe the thermal stratification in a solar storage tank. Also, Soliutis et al., [11] employed the ANN combined with the software TRNSYS in order to predict the performance of a Integrate Collector Storage prototype using as input data the month of year, the ambient temperature, global radiation, wind speed and incident angle to produce to produce the mean storage tank temperature. Finally Yaci and Entchev [12] predicted by ANNs the preheat tank stratification temperatures, the heat input values from the solar collector to the heat exchanger, the heat input to the auxiliary propane-tank and the derived solar fraction, for the solar thermal energy systems employed for hot water and heating applications.

For this reasons, the aim of this work is the development of a computational model employing ANN for thermal efficiency prediction (Eff) of a solar steam generation plant composed by a PTCs array, from experimental parameters.

2   Artificial Neural Networks

An Artificial Neural Network (ANN) is a structure inspired by the way the nervous system of animals works, and it is integrated by a number of interconnected units, called neurons (Fig. 1). This structure are used to estimate or approximate functions that can depend on a large number of inputs and are generally unknown; reason why ANN are considered nonlinear statistical data modelling tools and have been used in several engineering applications [13–15].

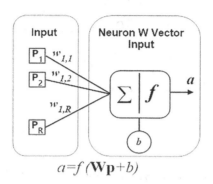

$$a=f\,(\mathbf{Wp}+b)$$

Fig. 1. Elementary neuron with R inputs.

An ANN can be seen like a black box in which enters a data base conformed by input variables. Each of the input variables is assigned with an appropriate weighting factor (W). The sum of the weighted inputs and the bias (b) produces the input for a transfer function which will generate an output value. The main characteristic of this model is that specific information of the physical behaviour system or the way in which the data were obtained are not required [16].

One of the more used ANN model is the known as multi-layer perceptron (MLP) [17] which can be trained to solve multivariable problems with nonlinear equations. The training process is realized by specific algorithms, where the most used is known as back-propagation [14]. The architecture of a MLP is usually divided into three parts: an input layer, a hidden layer(s) and an output layer (Fig. 2). At the training, the network learns from its errors until to get a model that describes with as much accuracy as possible the studied phenomenon. During the training, weight and bias matrices are generated which each iteration is modified until obtaining the optimal values [18]. At this work the transfer functions employed for nonlinear solutions are the hyperbolic tangent sigmoid transferfunction (Tansig, Eq. 1) and logarithmic sigmoid transferfunction (Logsig, Eq. 2) at the hidden layer; and a linear transfer function at the output layer [19].

$$Tansing(n) = \frac{2}{1 + \exp(-2n)} - 1 \tag{1}$$

$$Loging(n) = \frac{2}{1 + \exp(-n)} \tag{2}$$

$$Pureline(n) = n \tag{3}$$

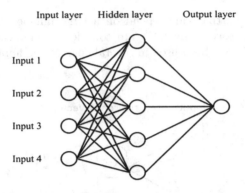

Fig. 2. Multi-layer perceptron neural network.

3   Solar Low Enthalpy Steam Generation Plant

The experimental database employed to carry out the present work, was obtained from a low enthalpy steam generation plant composed by a 2.44 m PTCs array. Figure 3 shows a schematic diagram of the system which operates with water as working fluid. The plant consists of two 120 L thermal storage tanks; two hp water pumps; several sensors for the measurement of temperature, pressure and fluid flow at various sections of the system; and an hydraulic circuit that allows to configure the plant for operation in two different modes, open circuit and close circuit.

The data acquisition of variables used for the predictive model development process was measured with average values at intervals of one minute according to ANSI/ASHRAE Standard 93 1986 (RA 91) which describe the assessment method for computing the thermal efficiency of a concentrating collector [20].

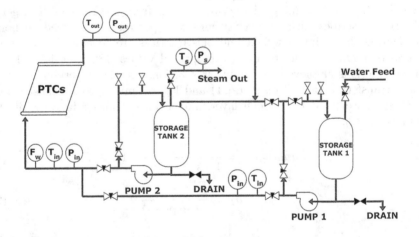

Fig. 3. Solar low enthalpy steam generation plant operation diagram.

The parameters measurement is divided in two categories: operational variables conformed by inlet temperature (T_{in}) and outlet temperature (T_{out}) working fluid, as well as flow working fluid (F_w); and environmental variables composed by ambient temperature (T_{amb}), direct solar radiation (G_b) and wind velocity (V_w). Table 1 shows the six parameters that form the database and the minimum and maximum ranges of each one.

Table 1. Parameters employed at the RNA prediction model.

Parameters		Min	Max	Units
Input				
Operational Variables:				
Inlet Flow Temperature	(T_{in})	27.75	86.30	[°C]
Outlet Flow Temperature	(T_{out})	34.70	100.2	[°C]
Flow working fluid	(F_w)	0.94	6.11	[L/min]
Environmental Variables:				
Ambient temperature	(T_{amb})	24.26	36.99	[°C]
Direct solar radiation	(G_b)	830.0	1014.0	[W/m2]
Wind velocity	(V_w)	0.95	3.98	[m/s]
Output				
Thermal Efficiency	(Eff)	0.16	0.63	[-]

4 Predictive Mathematical Model

The development of predictive mathematical model of the experimental database was divided in two parts, 80 % was destined to MLP learning and testing process and the other 20 % was employed for the validation of the results, in order to obtain a good representation of the data distribution.

At the training process, a normalized database, was entered into a MLP architecture, where the number of neurons at the input and output layers was given by the number of nput and output variables in the process, respectively. The LevenbergMarquardt (LM) backpropagation algorithm (which is a derivation of the Newton method) was employed to obtain the optimums weights and bias for the MLP model, due it is one of the most successful algorithms in increasing the convergence speed of the ANN with MLP architectures [21]. Once completed the training, a statistical comparison between experimental data and MLP training results is made, if it doesn't meet the criteria, the MLP architecture is modified and the training process is repeated. Figure 4 shows a schematic diagram of the numerical iteration of MLP training process described.

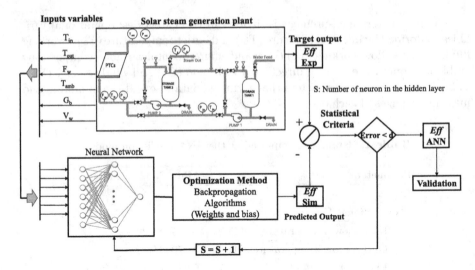

Fig. 4. Numerical procedure used for the MLP learning process, and the iterative architecture used by the model to predict the thermal efficiency in a low enthalpy steam generation plant.

4.1   Optimal ANN Architecture

In order to obtain the optimal MLP architecture, two different pairs of transfer functions (Tansig-Purelin and Logsig-Purelin) for the hidden layer and output layer were tested, varying the neuron number of the hidden layer. The Table 2 shows the results of statistical methods employed (Mean Absolute Percentage Error (MAPE), Root Mean Square Error (RMSE) and correlation coefficient (R^2)) [22] to each one of transfer function pairs with respect to experimental data.

Table 2. Results after training MLP

Neurons	T. Functions	MAPE	RMSE	R^2	Best L. Equation
1	*Tansig-Purelin*	6.3780	0.0343	0.83976	$y = 0.8393x + 0.0767$
	Logsig-Purelin	6.3784	0.0343	0.83974	$y = 0.8394x + 0.0767$
2	Tansig-Purelin	0.9107	0.0055	0.99606	$y = 0.9945x + 0.0014$
	Logsig-Purelin	0.7184	0.0045	0.99729	$y = 0.9956x + 0.0018$
3	*Tansig-Purelin*	0.3005	0.0017	0.99959	$y = 0.9984x + 7.26e^{-4}$
	Logsig-Purelin	0.4138	0.0024	0.99920	$y = 0.9988x + 5.36e^{-4}$
4	*Tansig-Purelin*	0.1831	0.0011	0.99984	$y = 0.9996x + 1.72e^{-4}$
	Logsig-Purelin	**0.0955**	**0.0006**	**0.99996**	$\mathbf{y = 1.0000x + 8.017e^{-5}}$

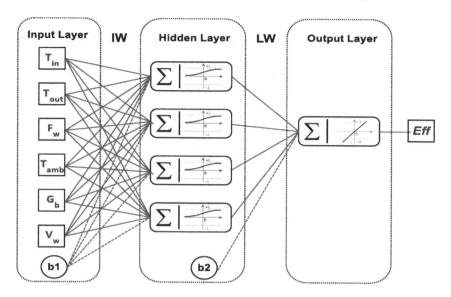

Fig. 5. MLP architecture for thermal efficiency prediction of low enthalpy steam generation plant.

As it can be seen the best MLP model prediction was obtained with 4 neurons in the hidden layer, and the transfer function pair Logsig-Purelin, generating a 6-4-1 MLP architecture (Fig. 5). This model present a smaller MAPE = 0.0955 % and RMSE = 0.0006; and the best linear behaviour fitting with respect to the experimental values given by:

$$Eff_{MLP} = 1.000 Eff_{Exp} + 8.017 \times 10^{-5} \tag{4}$$

where the slope of the equation (Eq. 4) is equal to the unity, and its ordinate is very close to zero, indicating a perfect linear fitting borne out by the determination coefficient value ($R^2 = 0.99996$).

The Figs. 6 and 7 shows a comparative between the experimental and simulated thermal efficiency values used at the training and testing stages, respectively. At both figures can be seen that simulated thermal efficiency present the same behaviour ($R^2 = 0.99996$) respect to experimental thermal efficiency independently if it belong to testing or training phase, indicating that samples selected for these process are representative of the phenomenon. On the other hand, through the axes of the graphs, it is possible to observe that the data base values employed covers all the measurement ranges, indicated at the Table 1.

The optimums weights and bias obtained for the best MLP model are shown in the Table 3; IW and LW are the input weights and output weights from the hidden layer; K and S are the total input (K = 6) and neuron (S = 4) numbers, and b1 and b2 the bias factor.

Therefore, based on the develop MLP architecture (Fig. 4); the logarithmic sigmoid transferfunction (Eq. 2); the linear transfer-function (Eq. 3);

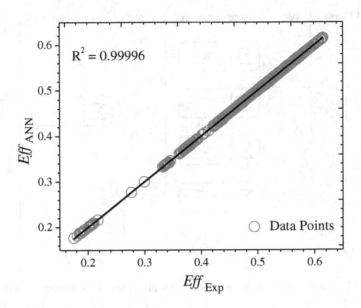

Fig. 6. Experimental versus simulated Eff values for the learning database.

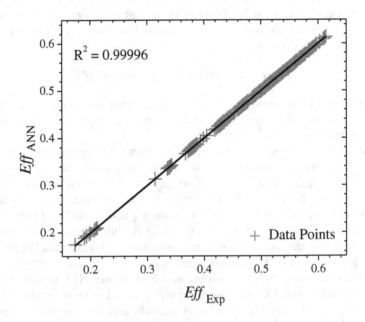

Fig. 7. Experimental versus simulated Eff values for the test database.

Table 3. MLP model prediction optimums weights and bias.

Neurons Number			1	2	3	4
Weights (W)	Hidden Layer S = 4 K = 6 IW(s,k)	T_{in} (k = 1)	−6.3264	−2.9117	−6.9882	9.5489
		T_{out} (k = 2)	7.2664	−2.4053	8.2889	−10.9960
		F_w (k = 3)	−2.0889	−6.7280	−2.1711	−2.9307
		T_{amb} (k = 4)	−0.2029	−1.1090	0.3753	0.2811
		G_b (k = 5)	−2.4611	−12.240	3.1826	4.0485
		V_w (k = 6)	0.0203	−0.7129	−0.0338	−0.0259
	Output Layer LW(s,1)	Eff (k = 7)	−3.0657	0.0441	2.0878	−2.0904
	Bias (b)	b1 (s)	−0.3510	21.1948	−0.7278	0.0081
		b2	0.3365			

and the values at the Table 3, the proposed model can be analytically represented by the following equation:

$$EffMLP = \sum_{j=1}^{S} \left[LW(1,j) \left(\frac{1}{1 + \exp(-(\sum_{k=1}^{K}(IW(j,k)in(k)) + b1(j)))} \right) \right] + b2$$
(5)

where LW, IW, b1,b2, K and S are described at Table 3, and In is the parameter value corresponding operation.

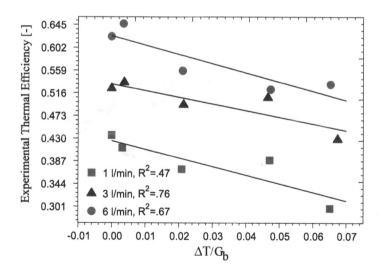

Fig. 8. Experimental thermal efficiency in function of the heat loss parameter for different work fluid flows.

5 Neural Network Validation

5.1 Thermal Efficiency and Heat Loss Parameter

The manner in which thermal efficiency is shown for a photothermal system is given by the ANSI/ASHRAE Standard 93 1986 (RA 91) [20]. This standard indicate that thermal efficiency must be plotted in function of a variable known as heat loss parameter ($\Delta T/GT_b$), where ΔT is the differences between the flow inlet temperature and the ambient temperature ($\Delta T = T_{in}\text{-}T_{amb}$), because this is affected by the solar radiation as well as the amount of heat that provides to

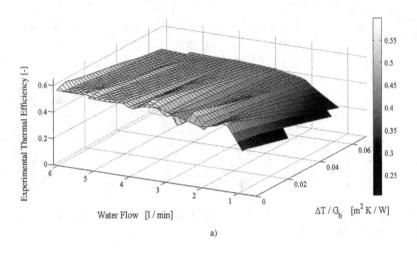

a)

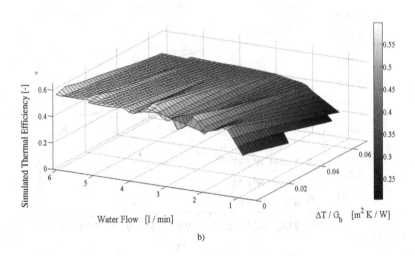

b)

Fig. 9. Thermal efficiency validation. (a) Experimental thermal efficiency not included at the MLP training. (b) Simulate Thermal efficiency from MLP model.

the system. The Fig. 8 shows the experimental thermal efficiency measurement at different working fluid flow values with its respective linear fits. At this picture is possible observe that the equation for each one of the working fluid flows is very poor at all the cases (as is suggested by their coefficients of determination), indicating that is no possible to solve this problem with a linear regression due this is a multivariable case and the equations not regard all the parameter that impact in the thermal efficiency.

5.2   Comparison of Experimental and Simulated Efficiency

The validation of the MLP model was carried out through a comparison employing data not included at the training process [23]. The efficiency comparison was made in function of two variables, the heat loss parameter ($\Delta T/Gb$) and the working fluid flow. Figure 9a shows the real behaviour of the thermal efficiency of the system in function of both parameters (heat loss parameter and fluid flow) and where can be seen a trend to decrease when ΔT increases. Moreover, Fig. 9b represents the values of thermal efficiency obtained from the mathematical model generated with MLP where an appropriate reproduction of the real efficiency curves can be seen, demonstrating that the model is capable of adapting to the variations of flow and heat losses as it is indicated in the statistical criteria from Table 2.

The results obtained after the model validation allows direct application to development cards destined to thermal efficiency prediction and estimation on line of the solar steam generation plant. On the other hand, the employment of this model can reduce research time and costs of system operation. Finally, the predictive model developed can be used to optimize the operating conditions of the arrangement of solar concentrators system.

6   Conclusions

A thermal efficiency predictive model of a solar low enthalpy steam generation plant was develop employing a Multi-Layer Perceptron Artificial Neural Network. The predictive model is presented like a simple computational mathematical equation obtained in function of six input parameters: inlet and outlet working fluid temperature, flow working fluid, ambient temperature, direct solar radiation and wind velocity. The neural networks model have been effectively train with experimental database and validated with an unbiased experimental database (considering the specified training range of operating conditions). The strength of the thermal efficiency computed is also carried out using statistical comparison between the stately and replicated values. Therefore, MLP model could be used for the consistent purpose of thermal efficiency in solar low enthalpy steam generation plants when the input variables measurements are well known into the training algorithms, creating the interactions without the need for a priori expectations about the nature of the connections between inputs and output variables. The progress of this model might have carried out the application of smart sensors for on-line quality assessment of thermal efficiency in solar low enthalpy steam generation plant. Besides, the model obtained allow a new research line employing the model as an objective function for the optimization of the system using heuristic and numeric computational models.

Acknowledgments. Part of this investigation was sustained by project: **PRODEP 2015 103.5/15/10486**.

References

1. Mekhilef, S., Saidur, R., Safar, A.: A review of solar energy use in industries. Renew. Sustain. Energy Rev. **15**, 1777–1790 (2011)
2. Solangi, K., Islam, M.R., Saidur, R., Rahim, N.A., Fayaz, H.: A review on solar energy policy. Renew. Sustain. Energy Rev. **15**, 2149–2163 (2011)
3. Kalogirou, S.A.: The potential of solar industrial process heat applications. Appl. Energy **76**, 337–361 (2003)
4. Fernndez-Garca, A., Zarza, E., Valenzuela, L., Pérez, M.: Parabolic-trough solar colectors and their applications. Renew. Sustain. Energy Rev. **14**, 1695–1721 (2010)
5. Bilgili, M., Sahin, B.: Comparative analysis of regressions and artificial neural network models for wind speed prediction. Meteorol. Atmos. Phys. **109**, 61–72 (2010)
6. Bhandari, B., Lee, K.-T., Lee, G.-Y., Cho, Y.-M., Ahn, S.-H.: Optimization of hybrid renewable energy ower systems: A review. Int. J. Precis. Eng. Manuf. Green Technol. **2**, 99–112 (2015)
7. Azadeh, A., Babazadeh, R., Asadzadeh, S.: Optimum estimation and forecasting of renewable energy. Renew. Sustain. Energy Rev. **27**, 605–612 (2013)
8. Raza, M.Q., Khosravi, A.: A review on artificial intelligence based load demand forecasting techniques for smart grid and buildings. Renew. Sustain. Energy Rev. **50**, 1352–1372 (2015)
9. Kalogirou, S., Panteliou, S., Dentsoras, A.: Modeling of solar domestic water heating systems using artificial neural networks. Sol. Energy **65**, 335–342 (1999)
10. Géczy-Vg, P., Farkas, I.: Neural network modelling of thermal stratification in a solar DHW storage. Sol. Energy **84**, 801–806 (2010)
11. Solioutis, M., Kalogirou, S., Tripagnotropoulos, Y.: Modelling on a ICS solar water heater using artificial neural networks and TRNSYS. Renew. Energy **34**, 1333–1339 (2010)
12. Yaci, W., Entchev, E.: Performance prediction of a solar thermal energy system using artificial neural networks. Appl. Thermal Eng. **73**, 1348–1359 (2014)
13. Haykin, S.: Neural Networks, 2nd edn. Prentice Hall, Cambridge (1999)
14. Demuth, H., Beale, M.: Neural Network Toolbox for use with MATLAB, User's guide version 4. The MathWorks (2014)
15. Kalogirou, S.: Artificial neural networks in renewable energy systems applications: a review. Renew. Sustain. Energy Rev. **5**, 373–401 (2001)
16. Bassam, A., Conde-Gutierrez, R.A., Castillo, J., Laredo, G.: Direct neural network modeling for separation of linear and branched paraffins by adsorption process for gasoline octane number improvement. Fuel **124**, 158–167 (2014)

17. Rumelhart, D., Geoffrey, E., Williams, R.J.: Learning internal representations by error propagation. In: Parallel Distributed Processing: Explorations in the Microstructure of Cognition, vol. 1, Foundations. MIT Press (1986)
18. Wasserman, P., Schwartz, T.: Neural networks. II. What are they and why is everybody so interested in them now? IEEE Expert **3**, 10–15 (1988)
19. Bassam, A., del Castillo, A.A., Garca-Valladares, O., Santoyo, E.: Determination of pressure drops in flowing geothermal wells by using artificial neural networks and wellbored simulaton tools. Appl. Thermal Eng. **75**, 1217–1228 (2014)
20. ANSI/ASHRAE 93–1986 (RA 91), Methods of testing to determine the thermal performance of solar collectors, American Society of Heating, Refrigerating and Air-Conditioning Engineers Inc. (1991)
21. Hagan, M., Menhaj, M.: Training feed forward networks with the marquardt algorithm. IEEE Trans. Neural Netw. **5**, 989–993 (1994)
22. Yadav, A., Chandel, S.: Solar radiation prediction using artificial neural network techniques: a review. Renew. Sustain. Energy Rev. **33**, 772–782 (2014)
23. Viuela, P.I., Len, I.G.: Artificial Neural Network Practical Approach. Pearson Prentice Hall, New York (2003)

Using Semantic Technologies for an Intelligent Medical Trainer

Gandhi S. Hernandez-Chan[✉], Edgar E. Ceh-Varela, Gimer Cervera-Evia,
and Victor Quijano-Aban

Information Technology and Communication School, Universidad Tecnologica Metropolitana,
Circuito Colonias Sur No 404, 97279 Mérida, Mexico
{gandhi.hernandez,eduardo.ceh,gimer.cervera,
victor.quijano}@utmetropolitana.edu.mx
http://www.utmetropolitana.edu.mx

Abstract. Diagnosis is the basis of medicine. Medical schools must evaluate
their students competencies in clinical reasoning in order to assess how medical
knowledge is applied by the student. It is also necessary that this knowledge is
available and shared by health professionals. For sharing and representing the
knowledge exist semantic technologies as terminologies and ontologies. Based
on an inference system we extracted from a medical knowledge base a list of
disease ontologies, and their related signs/symptoms and diagnostic test. We used
the cosine similarity metric to find closeness between diseases. A diagnosis
training module was developed, where a disease and its findings are shown to the
medicine student. Then, the student must select the corresponding disease from
a list of four possible similar diseases. Ontologies work great in the representation
of medical knowledge and its applications, however there is little evidence of its
uses on medical student training.

Keywords: Artificial intelligence · Semantics · Diagnosis · Medical training ·
Cosine similarity

1 Introduction

This paper presents a proposal of a computer system for medical training based on
semantic technologies. Intelligent systems need to use knowledge about things in order
to make inferences. In terms of Artificial Intelligence (AI), ontologies provide the
resources to formulate and make explicit knowledge in the form of a consensual vocabu-
lary [1]. Medicine schools are always looking for ways to assess the student knowledge.
Evaluation is always an integral part of medical education [2]. Many studies propose
new methods to evaluate the clinical competence of medicine students [3–5]. Competence in medicine refers to all knowledge, interpersonal skills, technical skills, and a set
of human characteristics that a medical professional must have in order to solve health
problems for the benefit of an individual and the community [5, 6].

Although several evaluation formats are used for the assessment of medical under-
graduates, questions with multiple choice answers are the most frequently implemented,
and these can be in paper or computer based tests [7]. These questions intend to evaluate

© Springer International Publishing Switzerland 2016
A. Martin-Gonzalez and V. Uc-Cetina (Eds.): ISICS 2016, CCIS 597, pp. 74–82, 2016.
DOI: 10.1007/978-3-319-30447-2_6

the knowledge and the academic improvement of medicine students. These questions are focused on the recall of knowledge and the application of that knowledge to solve a problem or make a decision [7, 8]. However questions must be well prepared in order to effectively assess clinical reasoning and how medical knowledge is applied by the student. Diagnosis is the basis of medicine, sometimes the diagnosis is obvious and sometimes it requires a complex clinical reasoning, either way, diagnosis is no error free [9]. In the United States the projected costs for 2019 as a result of medical errors are around \$4.7 trillion [10]. Another study [11] showed that a correct medical diagnostics can prevent for 44,000 to 98,000 deaths each year.

One way that medical students have to improve their diagnostic skills is the simulation of diagnostic cases. This improvement can be done using Clinical Decision Support Systems (CDSS), where the students can be trained to differentiate similar sets of clinical findings [12]. Although many CDSS exist, only one was developed with the primary intention of being a teaching tool. The expert system Iliad was developed by the University Of Utah School Of Medicine. It is used basically to train medical students to diagnose different cases [13]. Additionally there is another problem, in health care there are many different ways to express the same concept [14]. Although exist several vocabularies that are focused on to standardize clinical terms, for example: Read Codes, SNOMED CT (Systematized Nomenclature of Medicine Clinical Terms), or UMLS (Unified Medical Language System). Recently SNOMED CT has been used in CDSS and also well accepted in non-English speaking countries [15–17]. This paper presents a proposal of a computer system for medical diagnostics evaluation. The aim of this evaluation system is to help medical students to correlate clinical findings with a particular disease. The clinical findings are based on ontologies from a CDSS that use the SNOMED Clinical Terms.

2 Knowledge Representation

For the medical knowledge representation, in this experiment what is sought is to have reliable information and that somehow it is validated by the same professionals. It is also necessary that this knowledge is available and will be shared by health professionals in order to get better results from the CDSS (Clinical Decision Support System). For sharing and representing the knowledge there are two forms that are mainly used, and in some cases, created in a collaborative way, on the one hand are terminologies and on the second hand ontologies. Which are of interest for this research are those related to semantic technologies, for their utility in the field of representation of medical knowledge [18, 19] and the process of differential diagnosis [20–22]. In [23] the author states that medical terminologies play a key role in medical software. In fact they are part of the same software. The authors mention that it has been shown that traditional coding and classification schemes difficult to reuse and update knowledge. These difficulties have given way to new developments which allow divided the overall development of terminologies in three generations.

The first generation includes systems with hierarchical structures simple as ICD9 and ICD10[1]. The second generation includes compounds systems such as DICOM[2] from

---

[1] http://www.who.int/classifications/icd/en/.

[2] http://dicom.nema.org/.

SNOMED. The third generation includes compounds systems with automatic sorting, standardization and composed restrictions such as GALEN[3]. ONIONS [24] is one of the most important projects of terminologies of medical domain it has been applied to some medical terminologies as UMLS[4] [25], a large database of terms that has been populated through the integration of various sources including SNOMED CT[5] which is a terminology that has proved its useful in medical and health care context. It is a set of standards that was designed to be used by systems of the Federal government of the United States for the exchange of electronic health information and is also a standard required by interoperability specifications of the US Healthcare Information Technology Standards Panel. One of its main strengths is that it has also been accepted internationally as standard with other member countries of the IHTSDO. According with [26] SNOMED-RT and CTV3 (ClinicalTerms Version 3) are two controlled medical terminologies that have been joined to build SNOMED CT. SNOMED International has been developed for over 20 years and consists of more than 150,000 records organized into 12 different chapters [15]. These concepts include subjects of anatomy, morphology, normal and abnormal functions, symptoms and signs of disease, etc. With regard to diseases and diagnostics, many concepts have crossed to other concepts within the terminology references. Based on this, we decided to use SNOMED-CT to support the medical terms for the research. Another means of representation of medical knowledge that has been widely used by both professionals in health and engineers knowledge are ontologies which, by the nature of their structure based on propositional logic try to solve the semantic problems presented by the terminologies. The main use of Semantic Web technologies in medicine is applied to provide interoperability with existing systems, allowing the exchange of information [15]. Further, based on its capacity, the ontologies are very useful for knowledge representation, because they provide information systems with a semantically knowledge base for the interpretation of unstructured content [27]. Among the most known and used medical and biomedical ontologies, we can find OBO Foundry [28, 29], GO [30] IDO[6] MeSH and ICD [31].

Despite the large number of terminologies and ontologies existing in medical domain, we decided to use the one presented in [22]. In their work the authors presented a set of ontologies which was built in a modular architecture where a main ontology was created to define the relations among the subsumed ontologies. This ontology uses SNOMED-CT terminology to support and validate the concepts. The main reason for using this ontology is that, in comparison with the ones presented above, it allows a faster inference process because it was designed trying to be as light as possible, so it has no information that is not useful for diagnostic process. Figure 1 shows an example of a disease and its associated symptoms and tests.

---

[3] http://www.opengalen.org/ .

[4] http://www.nlm.nih.gov/research/umls/.

[5] http://www.nlm.nih.gov/research/umls/Snomed/snomed_main.html.

[6] http://infectiousdiseaseontology.org/page/Main_Page.

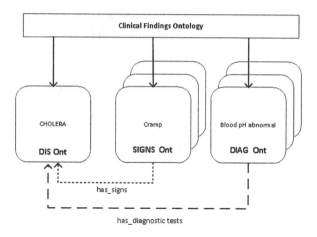

Fig. 1. Relation between a disease and its signs and tests.

3 Methodology

For the training process we have designed a training module that is part of the Medic-Us project. One of the main elements of this project is an inference engine which, in the training module, gets the name of a disease from a diseases list that was created randomly, and consults the knowledge base in order to bring back the findings related to the disease as a list of signs/symptoms and a list of diagnostic tests. So, the inference process in the training module comprises (1) the knowledge base that has the diseases information and (2) a set of inference rules. When a query is sent to the inference engine, it uses the Jena API[7] in or- der to obtain the knowledge that forms the medical case through the knowledge base and the inference rules. The Fig. 2 shows the architecture of the system.

Based on the signs ontology we extracted the diseases and their related signs and created a disease–signs dataset. It was necessary to find the closest diseases based on their signs in order to present to the medicine students four choices of diseases for them to choose the correct based on the list of signs presented. First, we implemented the technique of Bags of Words [32]. This technique is commonly used in the classification of text documents; however we used it on the disease-signs dataset taking each row containing the disease ID and its signs IDs as an independent text. The result was a dataset where each column represents a sign and each row represent a disease and a vector indicating if a sign was present or not. In total we had 225 different signs for the 30 diseases that forms our ontology. Secondly, with the new dataset and because its sparsity we use the cosine similarity distance algorithm in order to find for each disease which others are the closest. It outcome is always in the range of -1 and $+1$, the closest to $+1$ indicates the nearest distance between two instances [33, 34]. The cosine similarity between to vectors is defined as:

---

[7] http://jena.apache.org.

$$Sim\,(A,\ B) = \cos\,(\theta) = \frac{A \cdot B}{||A|| \, ||B||} \tag{1}$$

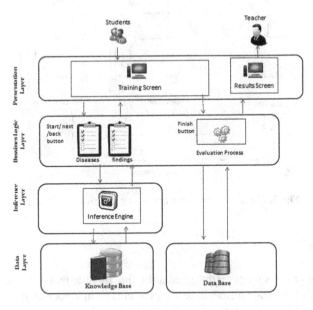

Fig. 2. Training module architecture.

Finally, we decided to use Principal Components Analysis (PCA) with the dataset for distance visualization. PCA allowed us to reduce the dataset dimensionality extracting the most important and relevant information and creating new features. These new features are lineal combinations of the current features and are called principal components [35]. These principal components are orthogonal to each other, being the first principal component the one with the most variance. The second principal component is orthogonal to the first and so on [36]. It is common to use one, two or three principal components to study the data structure [37].

```
Distance by: cosine                    |
I405737000 similar to I82272006
Pharyngitis similar to Common cold
Distance:  0.97
```

Fig. 3. Result distance between similar diseases.

Figure 3 plots the result of comparing the disease I405737000 with the disease I82272006. These IDs represent Pharyngitis and Common Cold and their distance in terms of the cosine similarity is 0.97. In Fig. 4(a), we used the first two components to plot the closeness of disease I405737000 (Pharyngitis) with disease I82272006 (Common Cold). Similarly, in Fig. 4(b) using the first three components we presented in a 3D model, the closeness of these two diseases among the others diseases existing in the ontologies implemented.

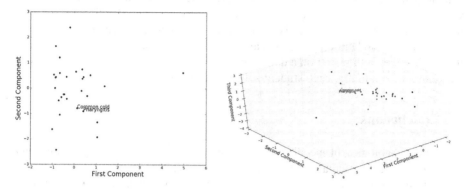

Fig. 4. Representation of diseases similarity

4 Results: Medic-Us Training Module

Figure 5 shows the training screen of the Medic-Us application. This screen presents two lists of clinical findings, the first list corresponds to signs/symptoms and the second list corresponds to diagnostic tests. When the student press the "Start Training" button the system create randomly a list of ten diseases and then take them

Fig. 5. Training screen of the Medic-Us application

one by one filling each list with the signs/symptoms and diagnostic tests related to each disease. The Options section show four answer options selected using the cosine similarity distance algorithm presented above. The "Next" button fills once more with the findings of the next disease in the diseases list. The "Back" button allows the students to go back in the list of diseases if they want to change an answer. Finally the "Finish" button grades the answers. The grade of the student is shown in the result screen and stored on a database in order to analyze the data. Due the lists are generated randomly, each student solves different cases.

5   Conclusions

Semantic technologies, in specific ontologies, have demonstrated great application and usefulness in the representation of medical knowledge and the development of software applications designed to obtain clinical diagnoses, however, there is little evidence of its application on developing systems for training medical students. Based on the importance of training, this paper presented the design and development of a software module supported by a part in the process of inference, for which it uses a set of ontologies, the SNOMED CT terminology and a rule–based inference engine, and secondly, the cosine similarity distance algorithm, so that the response options are chosen among a set of similar dis- eases to evaluate in a better way the knowledge of students. What is planned as future work is to request the participation of medical students in order to evaluate the effectiveness and performance of the training module.

References

1. Gandon, F.: Distributed Artificial Intelligence and Knowledge Management: ontologies and multi–agent systems for a corporate semantic web (Doctoral dissertation, Universit Nice Sophia Antipolis) (2002)
2. Schuwirth, L.W., van der Vleuten, C.P.: Different written assessment methods: what can be said about their strengths and weakness? Med. Educ. **38**(9), 974–979 (2004)
3. van der Vleuten, C.P., Schuwirth, L.W.: Assessing professional competence: from methods to programmes. Med. Educ. **39**(3), 309–317 (2005)
4. Collins, J.P., Gamble, G.D.: A multiformat interdisciplinary final examination. Med. Educ. **30**(4), 259–265 (1996)
5. Epstein, R.M., Hundert, E.M.: Defining and assessing professional competence. J. Am. Med. Assoc. **287**(2), 226–235 (2002)
6. Southgate, L.: Professional competence in medicine. Hosp. Med. **60**(3), 203–205 (1999)
7. Wass, V., Van der Vleuten, C., Shatzer, J., Jones, R.: Assessment of clinical competence. Lancet **357**(9260), 945–949 (2001)
8. Carranza, R.R.: La evaluación del conocimiento en medicina. Revista de la educación superior **37**(3), 31–42 (2008)
9. Croskerry, P.: Diagnostic failure: a cognitive and affective approach. In: Agency For Healthcare Research And Quality (2005)
10. Foster, R., Heffler, S.: Updated and extended national health expenditure projections, 2010–2019 (2009). [cited 27 August 2015]

11. Weingart, S.N., Wilson, R.M., Gibberd, R.W., Harrison, B.: Epidemiology of medical error. BMJ. Br. Med. J. **320**(7237), 774–777 (2000)
12. Reddy, K. Developing Reliable Clinical Diagnosis Support System
13. Lincoln, M.J., Turner, C.W., Haug, P.J., Warner, H.R., Williamson, J.W., Bouhaddou, O., Grant, M.: Iliad training enhances medical students diagnostic skills. J. Med. Syst. **15**(1), 93–110 (1991)
14. Dev, P., Hoffer, E., Barnett, G.: Computers in Medical Education, in Medical Informatics: Computer Applications in Health Care and Biomedicine, L.E.P. Edward H. Shortliffe, Editor. 2013, Springer Science and Business Media
15. Spackman, K.A., Campbell, K.E., Côté, R.A.: SNOMED RT: a reference terminology for health care. In: Proceedings of the AMIA Annual Fall Symposium. American Medical Informatics Association (1997)
16. Schulz, S., Bernhardt-Melischnig, J., Kreuzthaler, M., Daumke, P., Boeker, M.: Machine vs. human translation of SNOMED CT terms. In: Medinfo, pp. 581–584 (2013)
17. Maheronnaghsh, R., Nezareh, S., Sayyah, M.K., Rahimi-Movaghar, V.: Developing SNOMED-CT for decision making and data gathering: a software prototype for low back pain. Acta Medica Iranica **51**(8), 548–553 (2013)
18. Rector, A.L., Rogers, J.E., Zanstra, P.E., van der Haring, E.: Open- GALEN: open source medical terminology and tools. In: AMIA Annual Symposium Proceedings, p. 982 (2003)
19. Schober, D., Smith, B., Lewis, S., Kusnierczyk, W., Lomax, J., Mungall, C., Sansone, S.: Survey-based naming conventions for use in OBO foundry ontology development. BMC Bioinform. **10**(1), 125 (2009). doi:10.1186/1471-2105-10-125
20. Guefack, V.D., Gounot, V.B., Duvauferrier, R., Morelli, A.B.J., Lasbleiz, J.: Ontology driven decision support systems for medical diagnosis. In: Quality of Life Through Quality of Information, vol. 180, p. 108 (2012)
21. García-Crespo, A., Rodríguez-González, A., Mencke, M., Gómez-Berbís, J.M., Colomo-Palacios, R.: ODDIN: ontology-driven differential diagnosis based on logical inference and probabilistic refinements. Expert Syst. Appl. **37**(3), 2621–2628 (2010). doi: 10.1016/j.eswa.2009.08.016
22. Rodríguez-González, A., Hernández-Chan, G., Colomo-Palacios, R., Gómez-Berbís, J.M., García-Crespo, A., Alor-Hernández, G., Valencia-García, R.: Towards an ontology to support semantics enabled diagnostic decision support systems. Curr. Bioinform. **7**(3), 234–245 (2012). doi:10.2174/157489312802460721
23. Rector, A.L., Rossi, A., Consorti, M., Zanstra, P.E.: Practical development of reusable terminologies: GALEN–IN–USE and the GALEN organization. Int. J. Med. Inf. **48**(13), 71–84 (1998). doi:10.1016/S1386-5056(97),00113-5
24. Gangemi, A., Pisanelli, D., Steve, G.: An overview of the ONIONS project: applying ontologies to the integration of medical terminologies. Data Knowl. Eng. **31**(2), 183–220 (1999). doi:10.1016/S0169-023X(99),00023-3
25. Huang, K., Geller, J., Halper, M., Perl, Y., Xu, J.: Using WordNet synonym substitution to enhance UMLS source integration. Artif. Intell. Med. **46**(2), 97–109 (2009). doi:10.1016/j.artmed.2008.11.008
26. Wang, A.Y., Barrett, J.W., Bentley, T., Markwell, D., Price, C., Spackman, K.A., Stearns, M.Q.: Mapping between SNOMED RT and clinical terms version 3: a key component of the SNOMED CT development process. In: Proceedings of the AMIA Symposium, pp. 741–745 (2001)
27. Gruber, T.R.: Toward principles for the design of ontologies used for knowledge sharing? Int. J. Hum. Comput Stud. **43**(5–6), 907–928 (1995). doi:10.1006/ijhc.1995.1081

28. Smith, B., Ashburner, M., Rosse, C., Bard, J., Bug, W., Ceusters, W., Lewis, S.: The OBO foundry: coordinated evolution of ontologies to support biomedical data integration. Nat. Biotechnol. 25(11), 1251–1255 (2007). doi:10.1038/nbt1346

29. Mungall, C., Gkoutos, G., Smith, C., Haendel, M., Lewis, S., Ashburner, M.: Integrating phenotype ontologies across multiple species. Genome Biol. 11(1), R2 (2010). doi:10.1186/gb-2010-11-1-r2

30. Ashburner, M., Ball, C.A., Blake, J.A., Botstein, D., Butler, H., Cherry, J.M., Sherlock, G.: Gene ontology: tool for the unification of biology. Nat. Genet. 25(1), 25–29 (2000). doi:10.1038/75556

31. Cowell, L., Smith, B.: Infectious Disease Ontology. In: Sintchenko, V. (ed.) Infectious Disease Informatics, pp. 373–395. Springer, New York (2010). http://link.springer.com/chapter/10.1007/978-1-4419-1327-2_19

32. Provost, F., Fawcett, T.: Representation and mining text. In: Data Science for Business: What You Need to Know About Data Mining and Data-Analytic Thinking. O'Reilly Media Inc. (2013)

33. Nguyen, H.V., Bai, L.: Cosine similarity metric learning for face verification. In: Kimmel, R., Klette, R., Sugimoto, A. (eds.) ACCV 2010, Part II. LNCS, vol. 6493, pp. 709–720. Springer, Heidelberg (2011)

34. Zacharski, R.: A programmer's guide to data mining (2013)

35. Abdi, H., Williams, L.J.: Principal component analysis. WIREs Comp. Stat. 2, 433–459 (2010)

36. Boschetti, A., Massaron, L.: Python Data Science Essentials. Packt Publishing, Birmingham (2015)

37. Wold, S., Esbensen, K., Geladi, P.: Principal component analysis. Chemometr. Intell. Lab. Syst. 2(1), 37–52 (1987)

A Cloud-Based Intelligent Computing System for Contextual Exploration on Personal Sleep-Tracking Data Using Association Rule Mining

Zilu Liang[1,2,3]([✉]), Bernd Ploderer[1], Mario Alberto Chapa Martell[2], and Takuichi Nishimura[3]

[1] Department of Computing and Information Systems, University of Melbourne, Melbourne, Australia
{zilul, ploderer}@unimelb.edu.au
[2] Department of Electrical Engineering and Information Systems, The University of Tokyo, Tokyo, Japan
mchapam0300@satolab.u-tokyo.ac.jp
[3] Human Informatics Research Institute, National Institute of Advanced Industrial Science and Technology, Tsukuba, Japan
takuichi.nishimura@aist.go.jp

Abstract. With the development of wearable and mobile computing technology, more and more people start using sleep-tracking tools to collect personal sleep data on a daily basis aiming at understanding and improving their sleep. While sleep quality is influenced by many factors in a person's lifestyle context, such as exercise, diet and steps walked, existing tools simply visualize sleep data per se on a dashboard rather than analyse those data in combination with contextual factors. Hence many people find it difficult to make sense of their sleep data. In this paper, we present a cloud-based intelligent computing system named SleepExplorer that incorporates sleep domain knowledge and association rule mining for automated analysis on personal sleep data in light of contextual factors. Experiments show that the same contextual factors can play a distinct role in sleep of different people, and SleepExplorer could help users discover factors that are most relevant to their personal sleep.

Keywords: Association rules · Data mining · Personal informatics · Sleep tracking · Web applications · Health · Automated data analytics

1 Introduction and Motivation

The development of wearable and mobile computing technologies has made sleep-tracking (e.g., Fitbit, Jawbone, SleepAsAndroid, SleepBot) accessible for the general public. Individuals can collect personal sleep data with these commercial sleep-tracking tools in their own homes without having to visit sleep clinics. However, while collecting sleep data is becoming easier, making sense of these data remains a challenge. Existing sleep-tracking technologies generally focus on data collection and

© Springer International Publishing Switzerland 2016
A. Martin-Gonzalez and V. Uc-Cetina (Eds.): ISICS 2016, CCIS 597, pp. 83–96, 2016.
DOI: 10.1007/978-3-319-30447-2_7

only provide basic functions for data visualization, analysis and interpretation [1]. As a result, many users find it difficult to make sense of personal sleep data due to a lack of sleep domain knowledge as well as expertise in data analysis.

Analyzing personal sleep data is particularly challenging because sleep quality is influenced by many contextual factors [2, 3]. These factors could be grouped into four categories: physiological factors like body temperature and menstrual cycle, psychological factors like mood and stress, lifestyle factors like exercise and diet, and environmental factors like room temperature and exposure to digital devices. Understanding the relationship between sleep and contextual factors can provide actionable knowledge on what a person can change in order to sleep better. Previous studies show that the relationship between contextual factors and sleep is highly individual, implicating the importance of personal data analysis for each user rather than meta-analysis over aggregated data from a population sample [4, 5]. However, contextual exploration on personal sleep data for each user is not possible currently due to the lack of data analysis expertise and the lack of tools to support analysis. Existing sleep-tracking technologies rarely incorporate contextual factors in sleep data analysis regardless of the availability of those data. Furthermore, it is not feasible for many users to use professional data analysis software, as these tools were developed for experts and sufficient knowledge on statistics is required in order to use them [6].

To address the problems described above, we proposed and implemented a cloud-based intelligent system named SleepExplorer that incorporates sleep domain knowledge and association rule mining for automated analysis on personal sleep-data in light of contextual factors. A user simply needs to upload self-tracking data (including sleep data and contextual data), and SleepExplorer automatically conducts a sleep quality evaluation by referring to scientific standard. Based on the evaluation, SleepExplorer identifies associations between sleep and contextual factors using association rule mining. The identified associations provide actionable advice on behaviour change to improve sleep. We conducted a series of case studies using SleepExplorer and confirmed that the associations between sleep and contextual factors are highly individual. The users in these case studies gained new insights through SleepExplorer, and some of them used their insights to change their lifestyles in order to improve their sleep.

Based on our findings this paper offers the following contributions:

- We designed and implemented an intelligent computing system to help people explore their sleep-tracking data in light of contextual factors. The system integrates sleep domain knowledge and association rule mining to help users identify relevant associations between personal sleep and contextual factors, which can guide informed behaviour change for sleep improvement.
- We demonstrate how automated data mining can help individuals who do not have data analysis expertise to gain personal value from self-tracking data.

The rest of the paper is organized as follows. In Sect. 2 we summarize related work in sleep research and provide background knowledge on association rule mining. Section 3 presents the design and implementation of SleepExplorer system. In Sect. 4 we demonstrate case studies using SleepExplorer and discuss the main findings. We conclude in Sect. 5 with a summary and directions for future work.

2 Related Work

2.1 Sleep Domain Knowledge

Human sleep can be characterized along multiple dimensions, such as quantity, continuity and timing [30]. Sleep quality could be evaluated based on subjective perception (subjective sleep quality), and based on data measured using devices such as polysomnography, actigraphy, or accelerometer-based tools (objective sleep quality). In the field of sleep research and sleep medicine, PSQI (Pittsburgh Sleep Quality Index) [7] is widely used to evaluate average subjective sleep quality during the past one month. As for objective sleep quality, it is characterized by a set of metrics which is called sleep structure [8]. There could be connection between different sleep metrics within a user's sleep structure, and such connection could be highly individual [4]. Commercial sleep-tracking technologies could track a sub-set of sleep-structural metrics on daily basis, including minutes asleep, minutes awake, sleep onset latency, number of awakening, and sleep efficiency. According to [31], these variables are also the most relevant to sleep health.

It is suggested that both subjective and objective assessments of sleep quality should be considered because the two assess different aspects of an individual's sleep experience [32]. However, it is widely recognized in sleep research community that normal sleep is difficult to define because individuals vary enormously, differing in physiology, psychology, lifestyle, and living environment [9]. We conducted a thorough literature review in sleep research and sleep medicine, and identified the following threshold values for the five sleep metrics that wearable devices could track. We take this set of values as the population standard of normal sleep: minutes asleep being between 6 and 9 h [31, 33], number of awakenings being no higher than 3 times [34], minutes to fall asleep (also called sleep onset latency) being shorter than 31 min [35], and sleep efficiency being higher than 95 % [36].

2.2 Sleep-Tracking Technologies

Currently a large number of sleep-tracking products exist in the consumer market. The aims of these technologies cover various aspects of sleep: sleep inducing (e.g., White Noise1), dream journaling (e.g., Dreamboard), waking (e.g., Smart Alarm Clock), sleep tracking and environment monitoring (e.g., Hello Sense). The platforms of these technologies vary from mobiles (e.g., SleepAsAndroid, SleepBot), wearables (e.g., Fitbit, Jawbone) to advanced embedded tracking sensors (e.g., Beddit). They provide users with the information about how long they sleep, how well they sleep (sleep quality/efficiency score), the stages they sleep through, how to fall asleep and wake up with optimized freshness, and how to promote healthy sleep habits through sleep coaching tips. The mechanism of these sleep tracking devices and apps are similar to actigraphy which provides reasonably accurate results for normal, healthy adult populations [10]. These tools generally have two problems. First, users' sleep is not compared to population standard so that users do not know whether their sleep is normal or not. Second, contextual factors are not incorporated in sleep data analysis. This significant limit users' ability for sleep improvement, as simply make users aware of how bad they sleep is does not provide any information on how to solve their sleep problems. Liu, Ploderer and Hoang's [1] qualitative sleep study on sleep tracking technologies discovered that many users found it difficult to interpret sleep data without being provided with context and found no proper tool for laymen to conduct deeper analysis on the data.

In a framework of data-driven individual-level preventive health care [25], the authors emphasized the important role of health data analytics in converting self-tracking data to insights and actionable knowledge. Health analytics could be divided into multiple levels according to analytical capabilities [26]. Table 1 shows the mapping of analytics levels to sleep domain.

Table 1. Level of analytics in personal sleep-tracking.

Level of analytics	Techniques	Questions answered
Level-1 Analysis	Standard reports	−How was my sleep during the past days? −When did I sleep well/poorly?
	Ad hoc Reports	−How often I slept well/poorly?
	Query Drilldown	−Were there many awakenings during sleep? −Did I feel restless?
	Alerts	−Did I sleep too little?
Level-2 Analysis	Statistical analysis	−What are the factors that affect my sleep?
Level-3 Analysis	Forecasting	−Would I sleep better if I do more physical activities during the day?
	Predictive modeling	−How would my sleep quality be tonight? −What if I don't change my lifestyle, how will my sleep quality become as I age?
Level-4 Analysis	Optimization	−How should I change my lifestyle in order to maximize my sleep quality?

According to the above scale, most of the existing commercial sleep tracking technologies resides on level-1 analysis and only helps users understand "what happened", leaving the possible reasons and the potential counteractions unanswered. In order to answer these questions, higher level of analysis using statistics and data mining need to be conducted. We drew the implication from previous study and designed SleepExplorer to enable level-2 and part of level-3 analysis by integrating contextual information in sleep analysis, which will be discussed in the next section.

2.3 Association Rule Mining

Association data mining [11] aims to discover interesting relations between variables in databases and is a very important research topic in data mining. It was traditionally used for market basket analysis and was later applied to many other areas including web usage mining [12], intrusion detection [13], and bioinformatics [14]. Given a set of items I and a transaction database D consisting of subsets I, an association rule is a relationship in the form $A \overset{s,c}{\Rightarrow} B$, where $A, B \subset I$, $A \cap B = \varnothing$, s and c are minimum support and confidence of the rule. Every rule is composed by two different itemsets A and B, where A is called left-hand-side (LHS) and B is right-hand-side (RHS). The support of A with respect to the database D, denoted as $supp(A)$, is defined as the proportion of transactions in D that contains the itemset A. The confidence value of a rule $A \Rightarrow B$ with respect to D is defined as $\frac{supp(A \cup B)}{supp(A)}$. In addition to support and confidence, other measures of interestingness for rules include lift [15], all-confidence [16], collective strength [17], leverage [18] and so on. These measures are called objective measures as they characterize rule's structure, predictive power, and statistical significance. A comparison on different objective measures could be found in [19]. In contrast, subjective measures characterize unexpectedness and actionability of rules from users' perspectives [28].

Some well-known algorithms for mining frequent itemsets include Apriori [20], Eclat [21] and FP-Growth [22]. We build our algorithm based on the Apriori algorithm to avoid unnecessary complexity. Apriori algorithm uses a bottom-up approach for candidate generation. It generates candidate items sets of length k from item sets of length $k-1$ first and then it prunes the candidates which have an infrequent sub pattern. After that, it scans the transaction database to determine frequent item sets among the candidates. The algorithm terminates when no further successful candidates are found.

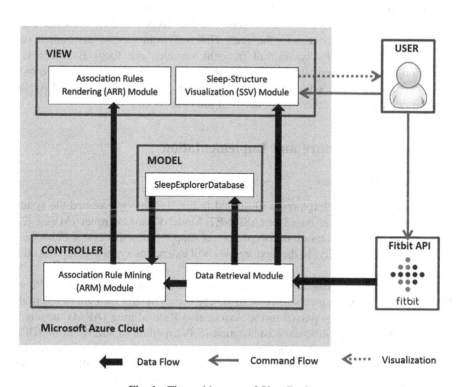

Fig. 1. The architecture of SleepExplorer.

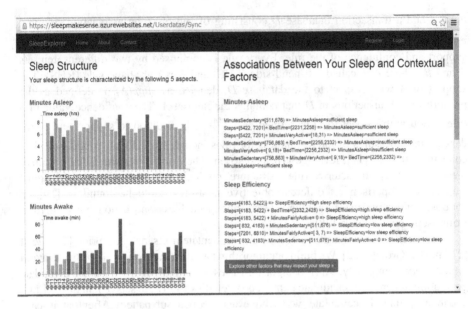

Fig. 2. A screenshot of SleepExplorer interface.

Since many users of sleep-tracking technologies are interested in understanding what contextual factors are associated to good and bad sleep, association rule mining is a promising technique to achieve the goal. Different from general association rule mining algorithms which discover all frequent itemsets, our focus is to discover association rules in a more structured manner so that users could identify the most relevant contextual factor set to their sleep. We therefore proposed a modified Apriori algorithm which will be described in detail in the next section.

3   System Architecture and Implementation

3.1   System Architecture

The architecture of SleepExplorer is illustrated in Fig. 1. We implemented the system on Microsoft Azure cloud based on ASP.NET Model-View-Controller (MVC) [23] framework. The current version of SleepExplorer support Fitbit devices as Fitbit has a wide base of users globally. In the next step we will extend the system to support other wearable devices.

SleepExplorer automatically retrieves a user's data from Fitbit public API via OAuth protocol upon the user's authorization. The retrieved data are then stored in the database as well as being passed to the Association Rule Mining (ARM) module in MODEL and the Sleep-Structure Visualization (SSV) module in VIEW. In MODEL, the ARM module performs the whole process of association rule mining including data cleaning, data discretization, and data mining. The mining algorithm will be described in details in the following subsection. Upon the completion of association rule mining, the discovered rules are passed to the Association Rules Rendering (ARR) module in VIEW. Eventually on the user interface (UI) a user would see his/her sleep structure plotted by SSV module using d3.js [24] and the discovered association rules rendered by ARR module. A screenshot of SleepExplorer UI is shown in Fig. 2. The left column visualizes the time series plots of each of the sleep-structural variables, and the days with bad sleep are highlighted using red color. The right column demonstrates the interesting associations discovered using association rule mining.

3.2 Mining Association Rules Between Sleep and Contextual Factors

Problem Definition and Objectives. The objective of association rule mining in SleepExplorer is to discover interesting associations between a set of contextual factors and sleep quality. The nature of the problem determines that the right-hand-side (RHS) of a rule can only include one sleep metric while the left-hand-side (LHS) of a rule is a set of contextual factors. In addition, it is not necessary for all sleep metrics to appear on the RHS. Our previous study [4] demonstrated that users tend to evaluate their sleep in terms of the sleep metrics that they were not satisfied with. For example, if a user suffered from interrupted sleep, he or she would quantify sleep quality in terms of the number of awakenings and thus fewer awakenings means better sleep for this person. On the other hand, for a user who had difficulty in falling asleep, this user would care more about how fast he/she fell asleep. This makes sense because psychologically people tend to pay more attention to negative events [29]. Based on our previous study, we infer that users are less concerned about the sleep metrics that always meet scientific standard and thus these variable do not need to appear on RHS of rules, e.g., if a user's sleep efficiency was always above 95 % then this user would be less interested in the rules related to sleep efficiency. Note that we could easily remove the above constraints and simply include all sleep-structural variables on RHS if a user was interested in all sleep metrics.

Let $T = \{T_1, T_2, \ldots, T_n, \ldots, T_N\} = \{\{X_1, Y_1\}, \{X_2, Y_2\}, \ldots, \{X_n, Y_n\}, \ldots, \{X_N, Y_N\}\}$ be a set of daily self-tracking data for N days, X_n and Y_n are contextual factors set and sleep data set tracked on day n. It is worth noting that in practice, N should be at least 10 days in order to produce any meaningful analysis results, and most studies on personal informatics collected data for more than one month. Contextual factor set X_n consists 9 variables that Fitbit automatically track: bed time $x_n^{BedTime}$, steps x_n^{Steps}, minutes sedentary $x_n^{MinSedentary}$, minutes very active $x_n^{MinVeryActive}$, minutes lightly active $x_n^{MinLightlyActive}$, minutes fairly active $x_n^{MinFairlyActive}$, intake calories $x_n^{CaloriesIn}$, water consumed x_n^{Water} and body weight x_n^{Weight}. Sleep data set Y_n consists four sleep metrics: minutes asleep y_n^{Asl}, number of awakenings y_n^{Nawk}, minutes to fall asleep y_n^{Mfs}, and sleep efficiency y_n^{Se}. We removed minutes awake as it is a redundant attribute of sleep efficiency. Good sleep is denoted as y_n^{XXX-} while bad sleep is denoted as y_n^{XXX+}.

The problem is thus defined as below.

Given

$$T = \{T_1, T_2, \ldots, T_n, \ldots T_N\} = \{\{X_1, Y_1\}, \{X_2, Y_2\}, \ldots, \{X_n, Y_n\}, \ldots, \{X_N, Y_N\}\}$$

Find

$$A^+ = \{A_1^+, A_2^+, \ldots, A_i^+, \ldots, A_I^+\} \text{ where } A_i^+ = \{X_i^{SUB} \overset{S,C}{\Rightarrow} Y_i^{SUB+}\} \text{ and}$$

$$A^- = \{A_1^-, A_2^-, \ldots, A_i^-, \ldots, A_I^-\} \text{ where } A_i^- = \{X_i^{SUB} \overset{S,C}{\Rightarrow} Y_i^{SUB-}\}$$

Constraints

$$y_n^{Asl} = \begin{cases} y_n^{Asl-}, 360 \leq y_n^{Asl} \leq 540 \\ y_n^{Asl+}, others \end{cases}, \quad y_n^{Nawk} = \begin{cases} y_n^{Nawk-}, y_n^{Nawk} \leq 3 \\ y_n^{Nawk+}, y_n^{Nawk} > 3 \end{cases},$$

$$y_n^{Mfs} = \begin{cases} y_n^{Mfs-}, y_n^{Mfs} \leq 30 \\ y_n^{Mfs+}, y_n^{Mfs} > 30 \end{cases}, \quad y_n^{Se} = \begin{cases} y_n^{Se-}, y_n^{Se} \geq 95\% \\ y_n^{Se+}, y_n^{Se} < 95\% \end{cases},$$

Where

$$X_n = \{x_n^{BedTime}, x_n^{Steps}, x_n^{MinSedentary}, x_n^{MinVeryActive}, x_n^{MinLightlyActive},$$

$$x_n^{MinFairtlyActive}, x_n^{CaloriesIn}, x_n^{Water}, x_n^{Weight}\};$$

$$X = X_1 \cup X_2 \cup \ldots \cup X_N;$$

$$X_i^{SUB} \subset X;$$

$$Y_n = \{y_n^{Asl}, y_n^{Nawk}, y_n^{Mfs}, y_n^{Se}\};$$

$$Y_i^{SUB+} = \{y_n^{Asl+} \mid \min_{n=1,2,\ldots,N} y_n^{Asl} < 360 \text{ or } \max_{n=1,2,\ldots,N} y_n^{Asl} > 540\} \text{ or}$$

$$\{y_i^{Nawk+} \mid \max_{n=1,2,\ldots,N} y_n^{NAwk} > 3\}$$

$$or \ \{y_i^{Mfs+} \mid \max_{n=1,2,\ldots,N} y_n^{Mfs} > 30\} \ or \ \{y_i^{Se+} \mid \min_{n=1,2,\ldots,N} y_n^{Se} < 95\%\}$$

I is the number of identified association rules.

Algorithm Flows. The association rule mining procedure implemented in SleepExplorer consists of three major steps. The first step is to remove non-interesting sleep variables, i.e., the ones that always satisfy the scientific standard. As it has been articulated in the previous subsection, we assume that users would be less interested in these metrics since their sleep was already very good in these aspects and there is no need for further improvement. The second step is to discover rules composed of frequent itemsets using Apriori algorithm [20]. In order to find the most interesting itemsets that mostly differentiate good and bad sleep, we use *lift* as interestingness measure to rank the rules in the frequent itemsets. The third step is to filter out the frequent itemsets for most interesting associations. The outline of the mining algorithm implemented in SleepExplorer is shown as follows:

(1) Remove unreliable entries: remove T_i if $x_i^{Steps} = 0$ or $x_i^{MinSedentary} = 0$ or $y_i^{Asl} = 0$ or $y_i^{Se} = 0$.

(2) Remove non-tracked contextual factors: remove $x_n^{Water}(n = 1,2,\ldots,N)$ if $\max_{n=1,2,\ldots,N} x_n^{Water} = 0$; remove $x_n^{Weight}(n = 1,2,\ldots,N)$ if deviation of $x_n^{Weight} = 0$.

(3) Remove non-interesting sleep-structural variables: remove $y_n^{Asl}(n = 1,2,\ldots,N)$ if $\min_{n=1,2,\ldots,N} y_n^{Asl} > 360$ and $\max_{n=1,2,\ldots,N} y_n^{Asl} < 540$; remove $y^{Nawk}(n = 1,2,\ldots,N)$ if $\max_{n=1,2,\ldots,N} y_n^{NAwk} < 3$; remove $y_n^{Mfs}(n = 1,2,\ldots,N)$ if $\max_{n=1,2,\ldots,N} y_n^{Mfs} < 30$; remove $y_n^{Se}(n = 1,2,\ldots,N)$ if $\min_{n=1,2,\ldots,N} y_n^{Se} > 95\%$.

(4) If $Y = \emptyset$, $A_{int}^{final} \leftarrow \emptyset$, go to (9); else, categorize sleep-structural variables as follows

$$y^{Asl} = \begin{cases} 0, & 360 \leq y^{Asl} \leq 540 \\ 1, & others \end{cases}, \quad y^{Nawk} = \begin{cases} 0, y^{Nawk} \leq 3 \\ 1, y^{Nawk} > 3 \end{cases}, \quad y^{Mfs} = \begin{cases} 0, y^{Mfs} \leq 30 \\ 1, y^{Mfs} > 30 \end{cases},$$

$$y^{Se} = \begin{cases} 0, y^{Se} \geq 95\% \\ 1, y^{Se} < 95\% \end{cases}. \text{ Discretize contextual variables.}$$

(5) Do Apriori algorithm to find frequent itemsets A that satisfies given threshold values of *supp* and *conf*.

(6) Filter $A_{int}^{Asl+} = \{A_a^+ | RHS = y^{Asl+}\}$, $A_{int}^{Nawk+} = \{A_b^+ | RHS = y_b^{Nawk+}\}$, $A_{int}^{Mfs+} = \{A_c^+ | RHS = y_c^{Mfs+}\}$, $A_{int}^{Se+} = \{A_d^+ | RHS = y_d^{Se+}\}$; ranking within each A_w^+ ($w = a,b,c,d$) according to *lift*, adding the top 3 rules in each set to the final rule set A_{int}^{final}. Abandon the rest of the rules.

(7) Filter $A_{int}^{Asl-} = \{A_a^- | RHS = y_a^{Asl-}\}$, $A_{int}^{Nawk-} = \{A_b^- | RHS = y_b^{Nawk-}\}$, $A_{int}^{Mfs-} = \{A_c^- | RHS = y_c^{Mfs-}\}$, $A_{int}^{Se-} = \{A_d^- | RHS = y_d^{Se-}\}$; ranking within each A_w^- ($w = a,b,c,d$) according to *lift*, adding the top 3 rules in each set to the final rule set A_{int}^{final}. Abandon the rest of the rules.

(8) Return A_{int}^{final}.

(9) End.

The *supp*, *conf* and *lift* of a rule $A_i = \{X_i^{SUB} \overset{s,c}{\Rightarrow} Y_i^{SUB+}\}$ could be calculated using the Eqs. (1)–(3).

$$supp(A_i) = P(X_i^{SUB})P(Y_i^{SUB+} | X_i^{SUB}) \tag{1}$$

$$conf(A_i) = P(Y_i^{SUB+} | X_i^{SUB}) \tag{2}$$

$$lift(A_i) = \frac{P(Y_i^{SUB+} | X_i^{SUB})}{P(Y_i^{SUB+})} \tag{3}$$

4 Case Study

Our implemented system has been tested with real-world self-tracking data which was collected in a field study from 3 participants [4]. Users synced the data into SleepExplorer database. The dataset from each user contains raw data on sleep and contextual factors for approximately 30 days. Each contextual factor was discretized based on frequency. We assume that if a pattern appeared more than 3 times in 30 days, it could be considered an interesting pattern. We thus set the threshold of *supp* to 0.10 (= 3/30). In the meanwhile we heuristically set the threshold of *conf* to 0.9. Therefore, only the rules that satisfy the conditions of *supp* $\geq$ 0.10 and *conf* $\geq$ 0.9 were added to the frequent itemset A. The automatic analysis results are shown in Table 2, where "[]" and "()" represents closed and open intervals respectively. As is mentioned in the previous section, the rules were ranked according to *lift*, and the top ranked rules (at most six rules for each sleep metric) were presented to the users in the form of "LHS → RHS". We decided to only present the top ranked rules to users rather than presenting an exhaustive list of rules, because our previous study [4] suggested that too much information on the user interface may overwhelm users and it is therefore important to strike a balance between the abundance and conciseness of information. In the study conducted in [4], many users mentioned that they were mostly concerned about the "top three" pieces of information.

There are multiple implications from Table 2. First, the effectiveness of SleepExplorer in discovering rules associated to good and bad sleep was heavily dependent on the characteristics of the dataset. Participant 1 and 3 generally had sufficient sleep and only suffered from sleep deprivation from time to time. Therefore in dataset 1 and 3 the number of entries for sufficient sleep was dominantly larger than that of insufficient sleep, which resulted in more association rules of sufficient sleep discovered. In contrast, participant 2 seldom had sufficient sleep, and the rules discovered were therefore mostly associated to insufficient sleep. The problem of imbalanced dataset needs to be addressed in future research.

Second, the distinct nature of associations identified for each participant suggested that the relationship between sleep and contextual factors could be highly individual. For instance, twelve hours of sitting a day was associated to high sleep efficiency for participant 3 but was associated to low sleep efficiency for participant 1. This echoes the correlation analysis results in [4] and suggests that it is important to understand how sleep is related to a person's specific life context in order to provide more efficient interference to their sleep problems. We also noticed that the rules in Table 2 were mostly the associations between physical activities and sleep quality. There may be two explanations for this. On the one hand, physical activities may be a most important association factor of sleep quality, which is supported by previous studies in sleep domain [37]. On the other hand, other contextual factors in the datasets may lack deviation to produce impact on sleep. In [27], the authors mentioned that routine activities and events did not have much relationship with sleep quality, because people already got used to these activities. In order to study the impact of these contextual factors, it is imperative to design rigid self-experiments according to the principle of N-of-1 trials [38]. This may require users to intentionally change routine activities in order to create deviations in contextual factors.

Third, the way how each contextual variable was discretized may impact how the results could be interpreted. For example, "MinutesVeryActive = [2, 6) ⇒ SleepEfficiency = low sleep efficiency" and "MinutesVeryActive = [6,18) ⇒ SleepEfficiency = low sleep efficiency" are two of the association rules discovered from dataset 2. These two rules could have been merged into one rule "MinutesVeryActive = [2,18) ⇒ SleepEfficiency = low sleep efficiency", which is more concise and informative.

In addition, we may also integrate domain knowledge when discretizing variables. For example, authorities recommend 30 min exercise every day. Therefore, we may use 30 as a threshold to discretize "MinutesVeryActive", and "MinutesVeryActive = [2,18) ⇒ SleepEfficiency = low sleep efficiency" thereby could be interpreted as follows: insufficient exercise is associated to low sleep efficiency for this participant.

It is worth noting that the current study have the following limitations. For one thing, the implementation of SleepExplorer could only investigate the associations between sleep and a limited set of contextual factors that could be tracked using commercial wearable devices such as Fitbit and Jawbone. As sleep could be affected by many factors [4], we will extend the functionality of SleepExplorer for easy tracking of other contextual factors such as caffeine consumption, alcohol consumption, electronic device usage, and so on. For another, we could not evaluate the automatic analysis results produced by SleepExplorer due to lack of ground true. In the next step we plan

Table 2. Association rules discovered from three sets of real-world self-tracking data on sleep and contextual factors.

Dataset ID	LHS	RHS	Lift	Supp	Conf
1	MinutesLightlyActive = [313,356]	MinutesAsleep = sufficient sleep	1.5	0.19	1
	MinutesVeryActive = [13,17)		1.5	0.19	1
	Steps = [12021,17010]		1.5	0.19	1
	MinutesFairlyActive = [4, 7)	SleepEfficiency = low sleep efficiency	1.17	0.19	1
	MinutesLightlyActive = [252,284)		1.17	0.19	1
	MinutesSedentary = [691,868]		1.17	0.19	1
2	MinutesVeryActive = [2, 6)	MinutesAsleep = insufficient sleep	1.03	0.10	1
	MinutesFairlyActive = [2, 4)		1.03	0.10	1
	MinutesVeryActive = [6,18)		1.03	0.18	1
	MinutesVeryActive = [2, 6)	SleepEfficiency = low sleep efficiency	1.03	0.10	1
	MinutesFairlyActive = [2, 4)		1.03	0.10	1
	MinutesVeryActive = [6,18)		1.03	0.18	1
3	MinutesVeryActive = [30,34)	MinutesAsleep = sufficient sleep	1.26	0.14	1
	MinutesSedentary = [725,803]		1.26	0.17	1
	MinutesSedentary = [602,633)		1.26	0.21	1
	MinutesSedentary = [696,725), MinutesLightlyActive = [198,236)	SleepEfficiency = high sleep efficiency	2.23	0.10	1
	Water = [710,1736), MinutesSedentary = [696,725)		2.23	0.10	1
	Steps = [13602,16777), MinutesFairlyActive = [17,40)		2.23	0.10	1
	MinutesSedentary = [725,803]	SleepEfficiency = low sleep efficiency	1.81	0.17	1
	Steps = [16777,18982], MinutesVeryActive = [49,63]		1.81	0.10	1
	Steps = [4559,10546), MinutesSedentary = [725,803]		1.81	0.10	1

to conduct a user trial and compare the analysis results in SleepExplorer with users' subjective observation of themselves. The effectiveness of the automatic data analysis using association rules mining could be validated if the analysis result is consistent with users' subjective perception.

5 Conclusions

In this study, we designed and implemented a cloud-based intelligent system named SleepExplorer that incorporates sleep domain knowledge and association rule mining for automated analysis on personal sleep-data in light of contextual factors. A user simply needs to upload self-tracking data (including sleep data and contextual data), and SleepExplorer automatically conducts sleep quality evaluation by referring to scientific standard. Based on the evaluation, SleepExplorer then identifies interesting associations between sleep and contextual factors using association rule mining. We conducted a case study where SleepExplorer helped three participants discover interesting associations between sleep and contextual factors. We found that such associations were highly individual, suggesting that it is important to consider a person's lifestyle context when interfere with his/her sleep problem. In the next step, we intend to extend the current study in three aspects. First, we plan to address the issue of imbalanced dataset and the discretization of variables integrating domain knowledge. We will also enrich the data mining routines in SleepExplorer. Last but not the least, we will conduct a user trial to evaluate the automatic analysis results in SleepExplorer with respect to users' subjective observations of themselves.

Acknowledgment. This study was supported by Australian Government Endeavour Research Fellowship and Microsoft BizSpark. We would like to thank Prof. James Bailey, Prof. Lars Kulik, Dr. Walter Karlen, Ms. Wanyu Liu, Dr. Yuxuan Li, Dr. Huizhi Elly Liang, and Mr. Yuan Li for their support and valuable feedback on this study.

References

1. Liu, W., Ploderer, W., Hoang, T.: In bed with technology: challenges and opportunities for sleep tracking. In: Proceedings of the Australian Computer-Human Interaction Conference (OzCHI 2015), pp 142–151, Melbourne, Australia (2015)
2. Mindell, J.A., Meltzer, L.J., Carskadon, M.A., Chervin, R.D.: Developmental aspects of sleep hygiene: findings from the 2004 national sleep foundation sleep in America poll. Sleep Med. 10(7), 771–779 (2009)
3. Poelstra, P.A.: Relationship between physical, psychological, social, and environmental variables and subjective sleep quality. Sleep 7(3), 255–260 (1984)
4. Liang, Z., Liu, W., Bernd, P., et al.: Making sense of personal sleep-tracking data through automated correlation analysis and visualization of sleep data and contextual information. In: Proceedings of the International Workshop on Healthy Aging Technology Mashup Service, Data and People, Shinagawa, Japan (2015)
5. Molenaar, P.C.M.: A manifesto on psychology as idiographic science bringing the person back into scientific psychology, this time forever. Measur.: Interdisc. Res. Perspect. 2, 201–218 (2004)

6. Ancker, J.S., Kaufman, D.: Rethinking health numeracy: a multidisciplinary literature review. J. Am. Med. Inform. Assoc. **14**(6), 713–721 (2007)
7. Buysse, D.J., Reynolds, C.F., Monk, T.H., Berman, S.R., Kupfer, D.J.: The pittsburgh sleep quality index: a new instrument for psychiatric practice and research. Psychiatry Res. **28**(2), 193–213 (1989)
8. Hublin, C., Partinen, M., Koskenvuo, M., Kaprio, J.: Sleep and mortality: a population-based 22-year follow-up study. Sleep **30**(10), 1245 (2007)
9. Closs, S.J.: Assessment of sleep in hospital patients: a review of methods. J. Adv. Nurs. **13**(4), 501–510 (1988)
10. Morgenthaler, T., Alessi, C., Friedman, L., et al.: Practice parameters for the use of actigraphy in the assessment of sleep and sleep disorders: an update for 2007. Sleep **30**(4), 519–529 (2007)
11. Agrawal, R., Imieliński, T., Swami, A.: Mining association rules between sets of items in large databases. In: Proceedings of the 1993 ACM SIGMOD International Conference on Management of Data - SIGMOD 1993, p. 207 (1993)
12. Cooley, R., Mobasher, B., Srivastava, J.: Data preparation for mining worldwide web browsing patterns. Knowl. Inf. Syst. **1**, 5–32 (1999)
13. Tajbakhsh, A., Rahmati, M., Mirzaei, A.: Intrusion detection using fuzzy association rules. Appl. Soft. Comput. 462–469 (2009)
14. Creighton, C., Hanash, S.: Mining gene expression databases for association rules. Bioinformatics **19**(1), 79–86 (2003)
15. Brin, S., Motwani, R., Ullman, J.D., Tsur, S.: Dynamic itemset counting and implication rules for market basket data. In: Proceedings of the ACM SIGMOD International Conference on Management of Data (SIGMOD 1997), pp. 265–276, Arizona, USA (1997)
16. Omiecinski, E.R.: Alternative interest measures for mining associations in databases. IEEE Trans. Knowl. Data Eng. **15**(1), 57–69 (2003)
17. Aggarwal, C.C., Yu, P.S.: A new framework for itemset generation. In: Proceedings of Symposium on Principles of Database Systems, pp. 18–24, Seattle, WA, USA (1998)
18. Piatetsky-Shapiro, G.: Discovery, analysis, and presentation of strong rules. Knowledge Discovery in Databases 229–248 (1991)
19. Tan, P.N., Kumar, V., Srivastava, J.: Selecting the right interestingness measure for association patterns. In: Proceedings of SIGKDD, pp. 32–41, Canada (2002)
20. Agrawal, R., Srikant, R.: Fast algorithms for mining association rules in large databases. In: Proceedings of the 20th International Conference on Very Large Data Bases (VLDB), pp. 487–499, Santiago, Chile (1994)
21. Zaki, M.J.: Scalable algorithms for association mining. IEEE Trans. Knowl. Data Eng. **12**(3), 372–390 (2000)
22. Han, J.: Mining frequent patterns without candidate generation. In: Proceedings of the ACM SIGMOD International Conference on Management of Data, pp. 1–12 (2000)
23. Krasner, G.E., Pope, S.T.: A cookbook for using the model-view controller user interface paradigm in Smalltalk-80. J. Object Oriented Program. **1**(3), 26–49 (1988)
24. D3.js data visualization library (2015). http://d3js.org. Accessed 26th December 2015
25. Liang, Z., Chapa-Martell, M.A.: Framing self-quantification for individual-level preventive health care. In: Proceedings of the International Conference on Health Informatics, pp. 336–343 (2015)
26. Kudyba, S.P.: Healthcare Informatics: Improving Efficiency and Productivity. CRC Press, Boca Raton (2010)
27. Choe, E.K., Lee, B., Kay, M., Pratt, W., Kientz, J.A.: SleepTight: low-burden, self-monitoring technology for capturing and reflecting on sleep behaviors. In: Proceedings of UbiComp 2015, pp. 121–132, Osaka, Japan (2015)

28. Silberschatz, A., Tuzhilin, A.: What makes patterns interesting in knowledge discovery systems? IEEE Trans. Know. Data Eng. **8**(6), 970–974 (1996)
29. Taylor, S.E.: Asymmetrical effects of positive and negative events: the mobilization-minimization hypothesis. Psychol. Bull. **110**(1), 67 (1991)
30. Hall, M.H., Okun, M.L., Atwood, C.W., Buysse, D.J., et al.: Measurement of sleep by polysomnography. In: Handbook of Physiological Research Methods in Health Psychology, pp. 341–367. Sage Publications (2008)
31. Buysse, D.J.: Sleep health: can we define it? Does it matter? Sleep **37**(1), 9–17 (2014)
32. Baker, F.C., Maloney, S., Driver, H.S.: A comparison of subjective estimates of sleep with objective polysomnographic data in healthy men and women. J. Psychosom. Res. **47**(4), 335–341 (1999)
33. Watson, N.F., Badr, M.S., Belenky, G., et al.: Joint consensus statement of the American academy of sleep medicine and sleep research society on the recommended amount of sleep for a healthy adult: methodology and discussion. Sleep **38**(8), 1161–1183 (2015)
34. Engle-Friedman, M., Bootzin, R.R., Hazlewood, L., Tsao, C.: An evaluation of behavioral treatments for insomnia in the older adults. J. Clin. Psychol. **48**, 77–90 (1992)
35. Lichstein, K.L., Durrence, H.H., Taylor, D.J., et al.: Quantitative criteria for insomnia. Behav. Res. Ther. **41**, 427–445 (2003)
36. Carskadon, M.A., Dement, W.C.: Normal human sleep: an overview. In: Kryger, M.H., Roth, T., Dement, W.C. (eds.) Principles and Practice of Sleep Medicine. 4th ed, pp. 13–23. Elsevier Saunders, Philadelphia (2005)
37. Chennaoui, M., et al.: Sleep and exercise: a reciprocal issue? Sleep Med. Rev. **20**, 59–72 (2014)
38. Kravitz, R.L., Duan, N. (eds.) and the DEcIDE Methods Center N-of-1 Guidance Panel. Design and Implementation of N-of-1 Trials: A User's Guide. AHRQ Publication No. 13 (14)-EHC122-EF. Rockville, MD: Agency for Healthcare Research and Quality (2014)

Fuzzy-Based Visual Servo with Path Planning for a Ball-Plate System

Chi-Cheng Cheng[✉] and Chin-Chuan Chou

Department of Mechanical and Electro-Mechanical Engineering,
National Sun Yat-Sen University, Kaohsiung, Taiwan, ROC
chengcc@mail.nsysu.edu.tw

Abstract. This paper presents a visual servo control scheme for a ball-plate system with a maze. The maze built on the plate forms obstacles for the ball and increases variety and complexity of its environment. The ball-plate system is a two degrees-of-freedom robotic wrist with an acrylic plate attached at the end effector. By using image processing techniques, the ball's position is acquired by the visual feedback, which was implemented with a webcam and a personal computer. A fuzzy controller, which provides dexterity of the robotic wrist, is designed to decide the slope angles of the plate to guide the ball to a designated target spot. Using the method of distance transform, the path planning based on the current position of the ball is conducted to find the shortest path toward the target spot. Besides, a relaxed path, appearing to be more suitable for actual application, is provided by the obstacle's expansion approach. Experimental results show that the presented control framework successfully leads the ball to pass through the maze and arrive at the target spot. The presented visual servo control scheme works effectively in both stabilization and tracking control missions.

Keywords: Fuzzy control · Machine vision · Path planning · The ball-plate system · Visual servo

1 Introduction

Traditional robots are usually applied for repetitive tasks, based on pre-programmed motion sequences. Although most assigned tasks can be accomplished for controlled environment, dexterity and flexibility to adapt to variable environment is required to build smarter robots. As a result, incorporating sensors into robotic systems to enhance autonomous capability in unknown and varying environment becomes the trend for new generation robots. Among all possible sensors, machine vision is the most popular technique to be chosen. Not only it is cost effective, but it mimics human eyes to acquire abundant information about surroundings.

Machine vision is a non-contact and non-destructive sensory way for measurement, inspection, and pattern recognition. Along with rapid development in microelectronics and IC fabrication, today's computers are able to perform mathematical manipulations for image processing effectively and efficiently. As a result, visual servo with image feedback becomes feasible. As long as a robot is equipped with a camera device, the

© Springer International Publishing Switzerland 2016
A. Martin-Gonzalez and V. Uc-Cetina (Eds.): ISICS 2016, CCIS 597, pp. 97–107, 2016.
DOI: 10.1007/978-3-319-30447-2_8

robot is able to conduct human-like vision-based dexterous behavior. In order to demonstrate performance of the proposed visual servo control framework with path planning feature, the ball-plate system is selected as the testbed.

The ball-plate system, an extension of the ball-and-beam system, is a typically multivariable nonlinear coupled dynamic system and has drawn researchers' attention for many years. Park and Lee proposed a sliding mode visual control method for a ball and plate system manipulated by a six degrees-of-freedom robotic arm [1]. In 2004, a language-driven control approach for a two degrees-of-freedom ball and plate system was implemented by Yip [2]. A hierarchical fuzzy control scheme consisting of three different fuzzy controllers was also developed for a ball-plate system in the same year [3]. Then a two-layer supervisory fuzzy control framework was presented with tracking performance evaluation on both square and circular paths [4]. A group of researchers worked on nonlinear control with output regulation to achieve position and tracking control for the ball and plate system [5]. Furthermore, a novel design of the ball and plate system accompanied by heuristic approach for image processing and a supervisory fuzzy control and sliding control scheme were also raised [6]. Although different control algorithms have been proposed, the visual servo concept has been widely applied in the ball and plate system.

This paper focus on incorporating fuzzy control algorithms and a path planning approach into a ball and plate system so that its operational dexterity can be enhanced to challenge the maze on the plate.

2   The Ball-Plate System

Figure 1 illustrates the framework of the completely developed ball-plate system, which mainly consists of a two degrees-of-freedom robotic wrist with a plate at its end effector and a webcam attached on a tripod. A ball (not shown) can freely roll on the plate. The webcam provides visual information of the ball and the plate. In order to demonstrate human-like dexterity of manipulation, different layouts of maze were also established on the plate. The control objectives are to guide the ball staying at a designated position or following a specified trajectory or reaching toward a target spot by solving the maze.

The ball-plate system is a highly nonlinear and coupled mechanical plant. Consider two coordinate reference frames, a global reference system $(O; X, Y, Z)$ and a body reference system $(p; x, y, z)$ whose origin P coincides with O, the origin of the former one as shown in Fig. 2. Assume θ_x and θ_y represent rotational angles of the body reference frame along x and y axes, respectively. The relationship between the global coordinates and the body coordinates can be formulated by

$$\begin{bmatrix} X \\ Y \\ Z \end{bmatrix} = \begin{bmatrix} \cos\theta_y & \sin\theta_x\sin\theta_y & \cos\theta_x\sin\theta_y \\ 0 & \cos\theta_x & -\sin\theta_x \\ -\sin\theta_y & \sin\theta_x\cos\theta_y & \cos\theta_x\cos\theta_y \end{bmatrix} \begin{bmatrix} x \\ y \\ 0 \end{bmatrix}. \tag{1}$$

The dynamic equations can therefore be solved by applying the Lagrange approach as follows:

$$\frac{\partial}{\partial t}\left(\frac{\partial L}{\partial \dot{x}}\right) - \left(\frac{\partial L}{\partial x}\right) = 0 \quad \text{and} \quad \frac{\partial}{\partial t}\left(\frac{\partial L}{\partial \dot{y}}\right) - \left(\frac{\partial L}{\partial y}\right) = 0. \tag{2}$$

The Lagragian L, defined as the difference between the kinetic energy K and the potential energy V of the ball with mass m and radius r, can be expressed by

$$L = \frac{1}{2}m\,|\dot{\mathbf{S}}|^2 + \frac{1}{5}mr^2\,|\boldsymbol{\Omega}_{\text{ball}}|^2 + mg(x\sin\theta_y - y\sin\theta_x\cos\theta_y) \tag{3}$$

$$V = mgZ = mg(-x\sin\theta_y + y\sin\theta_x\cos\theta_y), \tag{4}$$

where $\dot{\mathbf{S}}$ and $\boldsymbol{\Omega}_{\text{ball}}$, the linear velocity and the angular velocity of the ball in the global reference frame, can be obtained by taking time derivative of (1)

$$\boldsymbol{\Omega}_{ball} = \begin{bmatrix} \cos\theta_y & \sin\theta_x\sin\theta_y & \cos\theta_x\sin\theta_y \\ 0 & \cos\theta_x & -\sin\theta_x \\ -\sin\theta_y & \sin\theta_x\cos\theta_y & \cos\theta_x\cos\theta_y \end{bmatrix}\begin{bmatrix} -\dot{y}/r \\ -\dot{x}/r \\ 0 \end{bmatrix}. \tag{5}$$

Consequently, the final dynamic equations for the ball on the plate can be described by

$$\frac{7}{5}\ddot{x} - g\sin\theta_y + (2\dot{y}\dot{\theta}_y + y\ddot{\theta}_y)\sin\theta_x - x\dot{\theta}_y^2 + 2y\dot{\theta}_x\cos\theta_x = 0 \tag{6}$$

$$\frac{7}{5}\ddot{y} + \sin\theta_x(g\cos\theta_y - 2\dot{x}\dot{\theta}_y - x\ddot{\theta}_y) - y\left(\dot{\theta}_x^2 + \dot{\theta}_y^2\sin^2\theta_x\right) = 0. \tag{7}$$

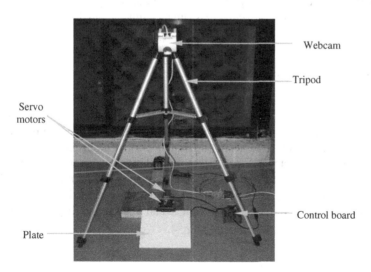

Fig. 1. The framework of the complete ball-plate system.

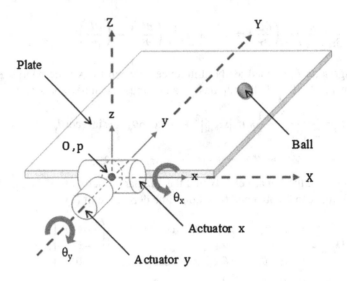

Fig. 2. Two coordinate reference frames for the ball-plate system.

3 Visual Servo and Path Planning

In order to guide the ball passing through the maze to the designated target on the plate, two major tasks, visual servo and path planning, have to be implemented. For the purpose of computational efficiency for actual experiments, time-saving but effective algorithm is the key concern.

3.1 Locating the Ball on the Plate

First of all, the position of the ball on the plate needs to be determined relying on visual information acquired by the webcam. If the region of the plate in the image can be obtained, searching efficiency for the ball will be greatly improved. In this paper, the region of the plate is resolved by searching for four corners of the plate along 45 degrees at image corners as depicted in Fig. 3. Since the ball has been given in advance, the ball can be easily acquired based on grey level of its surface. Furthermore, the position of the ball can be readily solved by finding the extreme pixels at the ball's boundary with maximal or minimal coordinate along both X and Y axes, i.e., $X_{ball(max)}$, $X_{ball(min)}$, $Y_{ball(max)}$, and $Y_{ball(min)}$, as illustrated in Fig. 4.

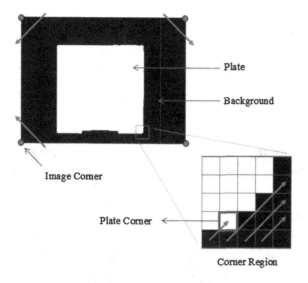

Fig. 3. Searching for corners of the plate.

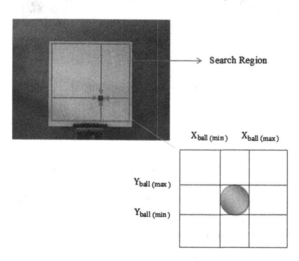

Fig. 4. Locating the ball on the plate.

3.2 Path Planning

Considering restriction for real-time implementation, the approach of distance transform was chosen for path planning due to its computational efficiency [7]. The idea behind this is to always follow the shortest distance measure based on a distance map generated by a ripple wave pattern starting at the target position [8].

At the beginning, the obstacle on the plate needs to be assigned as non-trespassing area. Then a distance map according to distance transform calculated based on the target position can be established as shown in Fig. 5(a). Apparently, in order to accomplish the mission of path following, the best way is just to track the path connected by locations with shortest distance. Nevertheless, the ball is actually not a point mass, but a circular region with certain area. For the purpose of actual implementation, before the distance transform is executed, the obstacle needs to be expanded. Figure 5(b) exhibits the final distance map, which provides a more conservative but more applicable path.

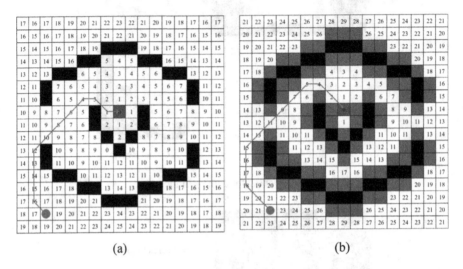

(a)   (b)

Fig. 5. (a) Illustrative path planning, (b) Path planning after obstacle expansion.

3.3 Fuzzy Controllers

Since fuzzy theory is close to human thinking, fuzzy control was chosen to implement the controller for the ball-plate system to mimick dexterous skills of human operation. Besides, the design approaches for both X and Y axes are exactly the same. Only controller design for X axis is presented here.

Define error function and its derivate along X direction as

$$E_X(t) = X_{t \text{ arg } et}(t) - X_{ball}(t) \tag{8}$$

$$\dot{E}_X(t) = \frac{E_X(t) - E_X(t - \Delta t)}{\Delta t}, \tag{9}$$

where Δt stands for the time increment of sampling. Standard triangular shape for membership functions is applied for easy calculation and operational efficiency. Figure 6 displays membership functions for θ_y, E_X, and $\dot{E}_X$ with the unit of pixel, pixel/s and degree. Forty-nine fuzzy rules in total were used to control the rotation along y axis and can be summarized as listed in Table 1. The Mamdani's method and the centroid approach were employed for rules inference and de-fuzzification, respectively.

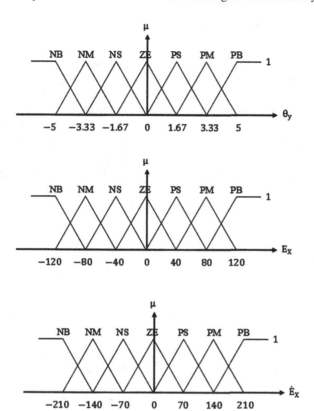

Fig. 6. Membership functions defined for θ_y, E_x and $\dot{E}_x$.

Table 1. Fuzzy associate memory for fuzzy rules.

θ_y \ E_x ___ $\dot{E}_x$	NB	NM	NS	ZE	PS	PM	PB
PB	ZE	PS	PM	PB	PB	PB	PB
PM	NS	ZE	PS	PM	PB	PB	PB
PS	NM	NS	ZE	PS	PM	PB	PB
ZE	NB	NM	NS	ZE	PS	PM	PB
NS	NB	NB	NM	NS	ZE	PS	PM
NM	NB	NB	NB	NM	NS	ZE	PS
NB	NB	NB	NB	NB	NM	NS	ZE

4   Simulations and Experiments

The experimental setup is depicted as in Fig. 1. The two degrees-of-freedom robotic wrist is manipulated by two small-size servo actuators manufactured by Hitec Corp. An SSC-32 servo controller developed by Lynxmotionm Inc. is chosen to drive those two servo actuators with the position resolution up to 0.1 degree by accepting commands through RS-232 interface. The plate is an acrylic square with edge length of 15 cm and thickness of 3 mm. The ball is 10 mm diameter steel ball commonly used for roller bearing. The webcam is a Philip SPC 300NC with an USB 2.0 communication standard. It provides 320×240 pixels image resolution and 30 fps for dynamic imaging capability. In order to implement path planning for the ball-plate system, two different mazes were designed on the plate as illustrated in Fig. 7. The height of the obstacle for the maze is 5 mm.

Fig. 7. Two different mazes applied to the experiments.

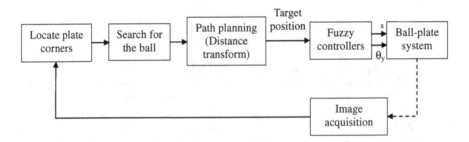

Fig. 8. Control block diagram of the proposed fuzzy-based visual servo scheme.

Figure 8 shows the control block diagram of the proposed fuzzy-based visual servo scheme with path planning for the ball-plate system. All software programs were developed in the environment of Borland C++ with the help of DirectShow SDK for image acquisition. Sampling frequency for both simulations and experiments were set to be 20 Hz for easy comparison. Three types of experiments including balancing, circular trajectory following, and path planning for challenging maze, were conducted for performance demonstration.

The balancing experiment was to bring a ball initially located somewhere on the plate to the center of the plate, where was (0, 85 pixels). Figure 9 illustrates the control performance with initial ball's position at (−50 pixels, 140 pixels). Both simulation and actual experiments exhibit similar and satisfactory control responses.

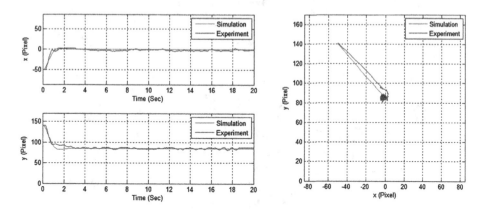

Fig. 9. Position control performance in the balancing experiment.

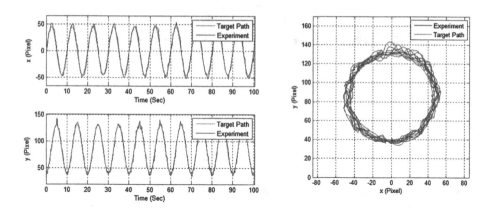

Fig. 10. Tracking control performance for following a circular path.

Capability to follow a given trajectory was examined by the tracking experiments. The given trajectory was a circular path with a diameter of 45 pixels and its center at (0, 85 pixels), where is the midpoint of the plate. Besides, the desired traveling period was 10 s per cycle. Tracking performance is demonstrated in Fig. 10. Apparently, the presented control algorithm successfully accomplished the designated tracking mission.

For the path planning experiments, the ball was initially put on a random position at the beginning. The goal is to manipulate the plate to lead the ball towards a designated target, either the center of the plate or the opposite spot on the plate. Actual paths of the ball to overcome the maze for different starting positions are displayed in Fig. 11.

The green crosses in the figure indicate the final target positions where the ball should be guided to. The experimental results show that the maze can be practically resolved by path planning using the technique of distance transform.

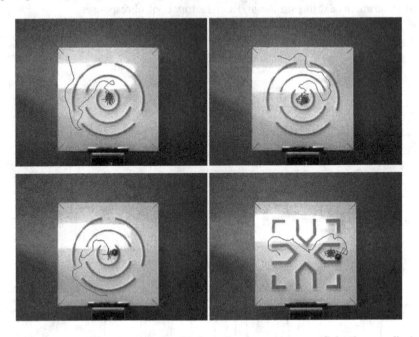

Fig. 11. Results of actual trajectories for the ball to traverse mazes (Color figure online).

5   Conclusions

Because of its multivariable nonlinear coupling characteristics, the ball-plate system was usually chosen as a platform for demonstration of visual servo control algorithms. This paper extends conventional balancing and trajectory following tasks to path planning for solving the maze on the plate. By incorporating the techniques of distance transform and obstacle expansion into the fuzzy control approach, the ball can be successfully guided to follow the shortest distance rule to the designated target position. In order to quickly locate the plate on the image plane, an efficient method to search for four corners of the plate was introduced. Since the theorem of fuzzy sets inherently tolerates possible uncertainties and parameter variations, robustness on control performance can still be assured especially with unmodelled dynamics and unexpected disturbances. Through extensive experiments on balancing, trajectory following and path planning for the maze on the plate, satisfactory control performance can always be achieved. Based on this preliminary achievement, further improvement and deeper exploration on related research topics can be carried on in the future.

References

1. Park, J.H., Lee, Y.J.: Robust visual servoing for motion control of the ball on a plate. Mechatronics **13**, 723–738 (2003)
2. Yip, P.T.: Symbol-based Control of a Ball-on-plate Mechanical System, M.S. thesis, Department of Mechanical Engineering, University of Maryland, USA (2004)
3. Fan, X., Zhang, N., Teng, S.: Trajectory planning and tracking of ball and plate system using hierarchical fuzzy control scheme. Fuzzy Sets Syst. **144**, 297–312 (2004)
4. Su, J., Tian, Y., Bai, M.: Research on trajectory tracking of ball-and-plate system based on supervisory fuzzy control. In: 2006 Chinese Control Conference, Harbin, China, pp. 1528–1532 (2006)
5. Wang, H., Tian, Y., Fu, S., Sui, Z.: Nonlinear control for output regulation of ball and plate system. In: 27th Chinese Control Conference, Kunming, China, pp. 382–387 (2008)
6. Moarref, M., Saadat, M., Vossoughi, G.: Mechatronic design and position control of a novel ball and plate system. In: 16th Mediterranean Conference on Control and Automation, Ajaccio, France, pp. 1071–1076 (2008)
7. Zheng, Y.F.: Recent Trends in Mobile Robots. World Scientific, Singapore (1993)
8. Gavrilut, I., Gacsadi, A., Grava, C., Tiponut, V.: Vision based algorithm for path planning of a mobile robot by using cellular neural networks. In: 2006 IEEE International Conference on Automation, Quality and Testing, Robotics, pp. 306–311 (2006)

Online Breast Cancer Diagnosis System

Asad Safi[1] and Anabel Martin-Gonzalez[2]([✉])

[1] Department of Computer Science, COMSATS Institute of Information Technology,
Park Road, Islamabad 45550, Pakistan
asad.safi@comsats.edu.pk
[2] Facultad de Matemáticas, Universidad Autónoma de Yucatán, Periférico Norte,
97119 Merida, Mexico
amarting@correo.uady.mx

Abstract. Breast cancer is the most common cancer among women,
and is the second leading cause of death after lung cancer. The ability to accurately identify the malignancy in early stage is the key for
better prognosis and preparation of effective treatment. In the developing world, even though at times imaging machines are available in
the rural areas but due to the absence of the relevant medical expertise
early detection of cancer remains only a pipe dream. Along with the
imaging machines, internet has made inroads into rural surroundings.
That makes the availability of online automatic systems that can identify the presence or absence of malignancy, without human involvement,
an important aspect of healthcare systems in the underdeveloped rural
surroundings. This paper presents an online tumor detection application, that uses mammogram images. The mammogram images taken at
a local facility are transferred over the internet to a remote server that
hosts the application that can classify tumour. It was trained on 322
mammographic images, from the mini-MIAS database. We have achieved
sensitivity of 90.15 %.

Keywords: Breast cancer · Classification · Supervised learning ·
Computer-aided diagnosis · Machine learning

1 Introduction

Breast Cancer is among the most frequent types of cancer and one of the most
malignant tumours among women [1]. The incidence of Breast Cancer in the
general population is increasing worldwide [2], due to ageing and lifestyle choices.
Its incidence has increased faster than that of almost all other cancers, and
the annual rates have increased at the rate of 3 % to 7 % in recent decades [3].
Breast tumour typically appears in the form of dense areas in the mammographic
images. A typical benign mass has a round, smooth and well restricted boundary;
on the other hand, a malignant tumour typically has a hazarded, uneven, and
blurry boundary [6,7].

Computer Aided Detection (CAD) systems can act in the supporting role to
a physician who has the final say. They can automatically detect and segment

© Springer International Publishing Switzerland 2016
A. Martin-Gonzalez and V. Uc-Cetina (Eds.): ISICS 2016, CCIS 597, pp. 108–115, 2016.
DOI: 10.1007/978-3-319-30447-2_9

tumorous regions from non-tumorous regions with a certain amount of accuracy, and can save time for the physician who can then suggest further testing and treatment [4]. The ultimate goal of CAD is to indicate such locations with great accuracy and reliability. Thus far, most studies support the fact that CAD has a positive impact on early breast cancer detection [13,14].

In the developing world, technology in the form of imaging machines has made inroads into rural and less developed areas with the para-medical staff that can use the imaging machines but do not have the requisite knowledge, expertise, and education to diagnose diseases from the images [5]. Also, internet has made inroads in those surroundings as well. Thus, automatic techniques may be helpful that can take images from the machines, transfer them via the internet over to a server that has the classifiers installed on it for tumour detection. This paper presents one such technique, with good results.

2 Breast Cancer Dataset

The original MIAS Database (digitised at 50 micron pixel edge) has been reduced to 200 micron pixel edge and clipped/padded so that every image is 1024 pixels × 1024 pixels [9]. The dataset list is arranged in pairs of films, where each pair represents the left (even filename numbers) and right mammograms (odd filename numbers) of a single patient. The size of all the images is 1024 pixels × 1024 pixels. The images have been centered in the matrix. When calcifications are present, centre locations and radii apply to clusters rather than individual calcifications. Coordinate system origin is the bottom-left corner. In some cases calcifications are widely distributed throughout the image rather than concentrated at a single site. In these cases centre locations and radii are inappropriate and have been omitted [9].

3 Proposed Approach

Our approach follows a typical machine learning methodology. In the first stage, image preprocessing is performed then we tackle automatic segmentation to isolate the breast from the background. Afterwards feature extraction is done from the image where they play the deciding role for classification into malignant and benign. In order to use only relevant features, feature selection is done based on the consensus among specialists on breast cancer. Once the features have been selected, labelled data is used to train a classifier. Cross validation has been used to ascertain the effectiveness of the methodology. In the following section we give details of each of these stages.

3.1 Preprocessing

Preprocessing is done to make the techniques extract more useful information from the images. The following preprocessing steps were performed which are

the work of Ireaneus et al. [15]: (1) The mammogram images were filtered by
using the Gaussian smoothing filter, which is afterwards used in standard deviation. (2) The morphological top hat filtering was performed on the grey scale
image and the structuring element is used. (3) The output is decomposed into
two scales using the discrete wavelet transform and thereafter the image is reconstructed [15].

To correct the uneven illumination the top hat filtering is applied if the
background is dark. To remove the uneven background illumination from the
images, the dark shaped structuring element is perform (Fig. 1).

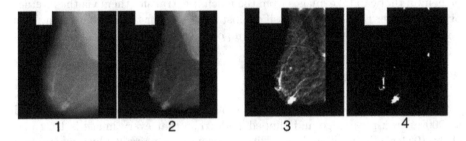

Fig. 1. (1) Original mammogram. (2) Filtered image. (3) Second level reconstructed
mammogram. (4) Tumor segmented output.

3.2   Segmentation

In order to segment the given image data we adopted the method as described
by Li et al. in [18].

Let $\Omega \subset \mathbb{R}^2$ denote the image domain. Then we define two soft-labeling
functions $u_{1,2} : \Omega \to [0,1]$ which can be used to define three soft membership
functions

$$M_1 = u_1 u_2, \quad M_2 = u_1(1 - u_2), \quad M_3 = 1 - u_1. \tag{1}$$

These membership functions provide a soft partitioning of the image domain,
because $M_1(x) + M_2(x) + M_3(x) = 1$ holds for all $x \in \Omega$, and allow us to segment
the image domain into three areas indicating healthy, bright parts of the breast,
and dark parts of the breast.

The described partitioning of the image domain is obtained by minimizing
the following convex energy

$$E = \frac{1}{2} \int_\Omega |\nabla u_1|^2 + |\nabla u_2|^2 \, dx + \lambda \sum_{k=1}^{3} \int_\Omega d_k M_k \, dx, \tag{2}$$

where

$$d_k = |a(x) - \bar{a}_k|^2 + |b(x) - \bar{b}_k|^2. \tag{3}$$

Here $a, b : \Omega \rightarrow \mathbb{R}^3$ are the gray scale space, while $\bar{a}_k, \bar{b}_k$ are the corresponding mean values:

$$\bar{a}_k = \frac{\int_\Omega M_k(x)a(x)\, dx}{\int_\Omega M_k(x)\, dx}, \quad \bar{b}_k = \frac{\int_\Omega M_k(x)b(x)\, dx}{\int_\Omega M_k(x)\, dx}. \tag{4}$$

The advantage of using the channels a and b of the gray scale space is that these channels only contain scale and no luminance information making the segmentation more robust with respect to inhomogeneous lighting conditions. For all experiments we chose $\lambda = 2$. Please note that using an approach which minimizes a convex energy allows for a fully automatic segmentation of the data.

3.3   Feature Extraction

The feature extraction is the key point of the classification and has to be adequate in order to obtain a good system detection rate. We selected a group of features which attempts to represent the characteristics observed by the Physician. We created a set of features trying to characterize them via computer vision techniques. The list of features selected is as follows: geometric, gray level, texture and shape properties. The properties obtained by the feature extractor are totally based on the segmentation step and the features have to be independent of the image (size, orientation, etc.) in order to be robust with regard to the image acquisition.

Geometric Properties: From segmentation of the breast, we obtain a binary image which represents the segmented blobs. Using this binary image, we get the bounding box and we fit an ellipse which has the same second inertia moment of area. Smaller blobs are erased from the binary image. Usually the biggest blob of the image is the segmented and the sparse small are only segmentation noise. The bounding box is our metric for the standardization of the breast. Using the bounding box and the fitted ellipse we reorient the breast to the biggest ellipse axis and we resize the image to a standard size. The features used to represent the geometric properties are as follows:

- **Relative Area:** Area of segmented with respect to the bounding box area. This area represents the size.
- **Relative Filled Area:** Area of the segmented with the internal holes filled w.r.t. the bounding box area. It represents how many internal areas of the were wrongly segmented.
- **Relative Centroid:** The centroid of the fitted ellipse w.r.t. the bounding box, indicating the distribution of the bounding box.
- **Eccentricity:** The fitted ellipse eccentricity which represents how circular is.
- **Solidity:** The relation between the convex area and the blob area, representing how irregular the border is.

We use the fitted ellipse and bounding box to **pre-process** the in order to create standard size and orientation to make the classification more robust.

The orientation always will be the same because we apply a reorientation based not only on the orientation of the ellipse, but also on the largest distance of the blob border with regard to the centroid. These properties allow us to reorientate the same with different angles to the same orientation. The bounding box is resized to a square using the largest side as the value of the square which is cropped and resized to a standard value of 100×100. This standard size allows to compare different sizes and orientation.

Gray Level Properties: The Gray level is very important in the classification because it encodes the variety. The histogram representing all the levels observed in the image [10]. The histogram is compacted in groups of values named **bins**. The bins allow us to reduce the number of 256 entries of a sparse histogram to a reasonably small dense histogram. The histogram is normalized with the total number of pixels used to create the histogram. In this way, we can compare histograms created from different sized images.

Texture Properties: This feature describes the differences between the allowing to characterize the discontinuity, which is a tool used by physicians to recognize if a malignant or not. To represent the texture, we use LBP (local binary pattern) of the image which creates a variability in the neighborhood of each pixel [11].

Shape Properties: This feature represents the shape properties, circular or irregular, which is a very important feature in the classification breast cancer. This feature is represented using histogram of oriented gradients (HOG) [12], which counts the occurrences of gradients in portions of the image, coding the variability of the gradient in the image. This feature represents not only the shape, but also the uniformity given the internal shape when the gray level changes, which is detected by the gradient. For each mammogram, 8 features are extracted with vectors size 53.

3.4   Classification

The goal of this stage is to classify the feature vectors in two classes: malignant and benign. A classification technique that proved very successful in our experiments are support vector machines (SVM, [16]). SVM was selected as the method of choice as it allows to linearly classify data in a high-dimensional feature space that is non-linearly related to the input space via the use of specific polynomial kernels [17].

The SVM classifier needs to be trained first before using it, thus we partition our input feature sets (y_i) $i = 1, .., n$, into two partitions, $T \subset \{1, ..., n\}$ the training set and $V \subset \{1, ..., n\}$ the testing (or validation) set with $T \cup V = \{1, ..., n\}$ and $T \cap V = \emptyset$. The training data set T is labeled manually into two classes using the ground truth, $l(y_i) = \pm 1$. Once the classifier is trained, a simple evaluation of the decision function $d(y_i) = \pm 1$ will yield the classification of any data y_i.

In detail, SVM is trying to separate the data $\phi(y_i)$ mapped by the selected kernel function ϕ by a hyperplane $w^T\phi(y_i) + b = 0$ with w the normal vector and b the translation. The decision function then is $d(y_i) = \text{sgn}(w^T\phi(y_i) + b)$. Maximizing the margin and introducing slack variables $\xi = (\xi_i)$ for non-separable data, we receive the primal optimization problem:

$$\min_{w,b,\xi} = \frac{1}{2}w^T w + C\sum_{i \in T} \xi_i \qquad (5)$$

with constraints $l(y_i)(w^t\phi(y_i) + b) \geq 1 - \xi_i$, $\xi \geq 0$ for $i \in T$. C is a user-determined penalty parameter. Switching to the dual optimization problem allows for easier computation,

$$\min_{\alpha} = \frac{1}{2}\alpha^T Q\alpha - e^T\alpha \qquad (6)$$

with constraints $0 \leq \alpha_i \leq C$ for $i \in T$, $\sum_{i \in T} y_i\alpha_i = 0$. The $\alpha = (\alpha_i)$ are the so-called support vectors, $e = [1, ...1]^T$ and Q is the positive semidefinite matrix formed by $Q_{jk} = l(y_j)l(y_k)K(y_j, y_k)$, and $K(y_j, y_k) = \phi(y_j)^T \phi(y_k)$ is the kernel function built from ϕ. Once this optimization problem is solved, we determine the hyperplane parameters w and b, w directly as $w = \sum_{i \in T} \alpha_i l(y_i)\phi(y_i)$ and b via one of the Karush-Kuhn-Tucker conditions as $b = -l(y_i)y_i^T w$, for those i with $0 < \alpha_i < C$. Thus the decision function of the trained SVM classifier ends up as

$$d(y_i) = \text{sgn}\big(w^T\phi(y_i) + b\big) = \text{sgn}\left(\sum_{j \in T} \alpha_i l(y_i)K(y_j, y_i) + b\right). \qquad (7)$$

4 Results

Performance evaluation was conducted using a 10-fold cross-validation. The 10-fold cross-validation gives an approximation of the general classifier performance. We created 10 balanced data sets which were generated from the original unbalanced data set of benign and malignant. The balanced data sets were generated by selecting randomly a similar number of benign and malign images to obtain a more general and balanced training dataset. We assess the feature training and perform 10-fold cross-validation utilizing the 10 balanced datasets. The results of these data sets are shown in Table 1.

The results show a very good performance in all the random data sets, allowing us to conclude that the selected feature vector gives meaningful information for the classification. The correctly classified instances value indicates a performance over 90 % in all 10 tested cases. If we observe only the malignant classification, which is the most important, the performance shows a true positives

Table 1. Results of the 10 random balanced data sets, and for each dataset 10-fold cross-validation using a SVM classifier (Avg-Std 90.54414 ± 0.045317).

Variables	Test-1	Test-2	Test-3	Test-4	Test-5
Correctly Classified Instances	90.5772 %	90.5743 %	87.5765 %	86.5614 %	87.5167 %
Incorrectly Classified Instances	1.4228 %	1.4257 %	1.4235 %	1.4386 %	1.4833 %
True Positives Rate	0.991 %	0.996 %	0.993 %	0.997 %	0.995 %
False Positives Rate	0.019 %	0.023 %	0.034 %	0.025 %	0.021 %
Variables	Test-6	Test-7	Test-8	Test-9	Test-10
Correctly Classified Instances	90.4982 %	90.5765 %	89.5965 %	88.4624 %	90.5017 %
Incorrectly Classified Instances	1.5018 %	1.4235 %	1.4235 %	1.5376 %	1.4983 %
True Positives Rate	0.981 %	0.991 %	0.983 %	0.991 %	0.996 %
False Positives Rate	0.059 %	0.033 %	0.064 %	0.020 %	0.13 %

rate greater than 90 %, meaning that the classifier recognizes as malignant 90 %. Therefore, the number of malignant which are not correctly classified is 10 %.

In the literature breast cancer diagnosis research are abundance, and most of them reported high classification accuracies. In the research work of Albrecht et al. (2002) [22], a learning algorithm that combined logarithmic simulated annealing with the perceptron algorithm was used and the reported accuracy was 98.8 %. In Abonyi et al. (2003) [21], an accuracy of 95.57 % was obtained with the application of supervised fuzzy clustering technique. In the work of Polat et al. (2007) [19], least square SVM was used and an accuracy of 98.53 % was obtained. Goodman et al. (2002) [20] applied three different methods to the problem which were resulted with the following accuracies: optimized-LVQ methods performance was 96.7 %, big-LVQ method reached 96.8 % and the last method, AIRS, which proposed depending on the artificial immune system, obtained 97.2 % classification accuracy. Abonyi and Szeifert (2003) [21] applied supervised fuzzy clustering (SFC) technique and obtained 95.57 % accuracy.

The accuracy results of the literaure review are far better than the result of this article, to have much batter results are the next the extension of the this research in future. The main target of this research paper was to have the base for online system, which is practical in underdeveloped countries. The system is tested and 9 out of 11 suburban hospitals participate in the experiment. The classification results will be improved in near future.

References

1. Smith, R.A.: Breast cancer screening among women younger than age 50: a current assessment of the issues. CA Cancer J. Clin. **50**, 312–336 (2000)
2. Parkin, D.M., Bray, F., Ferlay, J., Pisani, P.: Global cancer statistics, 2002. CA Cancer J. Clin. **55**, 74–108 (2005)
3. Stewart, B., Kleihues, P.E.: World Cancer Report. IARC Press, Lyon (2003)
4. Executive summary of the national cancer control programmes: policies and managerial guidelines. World Health Organization, Geneva (2002)
5. Pal, S.K., Mittal, B.: Fight against cancer in countries with limited resources: the post-genomic era scenario. Asian Pac. J. Cancer Prev. **5**, 328–333 (2004)
6. Fear, E.C., Meaney, P.M., Stuchly, M.A.: Microwaves for breast cancer detection. IEEE Potentials **22**, 12–18 (2003)
7. Homer, M.J.: Mammographic Interpretation: A Practical Approach, 2nd edn. McGraw Hill, Boston (1997)
8. Cortes, C., Vapnik, V.: Support-vector networks. Mach. Learn. **20**(3), 273–297 (1995)
9. Suckling, J., Boggis, C.R.M., Hutt, I.: The Mammographic Image Analysis Society Digital Mammogram Database. In: Exerpta Medica. International Congress Series, vol. 1069, pp. 375–378 (1994)
10. Kapur, J.N., Sahoo, P.K., Wong, A.K.C.: A new method for gray-level picture thresholding using the entropy of the histogram. Comput. Vis. Graph. Image Process. **29**(3), 273–285 (1985)
11. Maenpaa, T.: The Local binary pattern approach to texture analysis: extenxions and applications. Oulun yliopisto (2003)
12. Tsai, G.: Histogram of oriented gradients. University of Michigan (2010)
13. Burhenne, L.J.W.: Potential contribution of computer aided detection to the sensitivity of screening mammography. Radiology **215**, 554–562 (2000)
14. Freer, T.W., Ulissey, M.J.: Screening mammography with computer aided detection: prospective study of 2860 patients in a community breast cancer. Radiology **220**, 781–786 (2001)
15. Ireaneus Anna Rejani, Y., et al.: Early detection of breast cancer using SVM classifier technique. Int. J. Comput. Sci. Eng. **1**(3), 127–130 (2009)
16. Cristianini, N., Shawe-Taylor, J.: An Introduction to Support Vector Machines and Other Kernel-Based Learning Methods. Cambridge University Press, Cambridge (2000). ISBN:0521780195
17. Schlkopf, B., Smola, A.J.: Learning with Kernels: Support Vector Machines, Regularization, Optimization, and Beyond. The MIT Press, Cambridge (2001)
18. Li, F., Shen, C., Li, C.: Multiphase soft segmentation with total variation and H1 regularization. J. Math. Imag. Vis. **37**(2), 98–111 (2010)
19. Polat, K., Gunes, S.: Breast cancer diagnosis using least square support vector machine. Digital Signal Process. **17**(4), 694–701 (2007)
20. Goodman, D.E., Boggess, L., Watkins, A.: Artificial immune system classification of multiple-class problems. In: Proceedings of the Artificial Neural Networks in Engineering ANNIE 2002, pp. 179–183 (2002)
21. Abonyi, J., Szeifert, F.: Supervised fuzzy clustering for the identification of fuzzy classifiers. Pattern Recogn. Lett. **14**(24), 2195–2207 (2003)
22. Albrecht, A.A., Lappas, G., Vinterbo, S.A., Wong, C.K., Ohno-Machado, L.: Two applications of the LSA machine. In: Proceedings of the 9th International Conference on Neural Information Processing, pp. 184–189 (2002)

Recognizing Motion Images Solid Waste Jumbled on a Neural Network with a Simple Tracking Performed in an Automatic and Robotic Recycling Line

Martín García-Hernández[1](✉), Alejandro Flores[2], Eleazar Elizalde[2], Alejandro J. García-Arredondo[3], Miguel A. Gutiérrez-Muro[3], and Nidiyare Hevia-Montiel[4]

[1] System and Technology, CreoReal, 45030 Zapopan, Jalisco, Mexico
`martino@creoreal.com`
[2] Technology Division, Ingenia 4TI, Zapopan, Jalisco, Mexico
[3] Information Technology Management, Electronics and Control, CIATEQ A.C., 20358 Aguascalientes, Mexico
[4] IIMAS - UNAM, 97000 Merida, Yucatan, Mexico

Abstract. In this paper, we show the vision system in recognition motion images and detection of solid urban waste (SUW) and their integration on an automatic robotic line with a simple tracking algorithm. The detection and image processing are able to detect, identify and calculate the position of the SUW and send the coordinates to a delta robot for selection. The image processing system is previously trained in a neural network. Delta robots are provided by ABB Corporation and have been programmed to select the SUW through a simple algorithm to tracking. We present the integration of these systems and we describe the automatic and robotic machine with the vision system.

Keywords: Vision detection system · Neural networks · Image processing · Delta robotic · Tracking algorithm · Solid Urban Waste (SUW)

1 Introduction

Several applications emerged from the motion images recognition, and many of them applied to face recognition [1], human actions [2] and other approaches and techniques [3] such as artificial vision [4]. In this context, we develop, integrate and system identification and image recognition to SUW with a purpose built automatic and robotic recycling line.

The problem of SUW has increased with the rapid growth of factories and population in big cities. In Mexico, for 112,500 tons of SUW generated daily, the estimated potential recovery is: cardboard and paper 70 % y 45 % respectively, plastics waste 55 %, recycled aluminum 60 % and glass waste 75 % [5]. In this perspective, we implement a vision system to detect the main recyclable SUW

A. Martin-Gonzalez and V. Uc-Cetina (Eds.): ISICS 2016, CCIS 597, pp. 116–124, 2016.
DOI: 10.1007/978-3-319-30447-2_10

and we develop, build, programmed and integrated in an automated and robotic recycling line.

This paper is organized as follows. In Sect. 2, we introduce the motion images recognition system and detection of SUW. Section 3, presents an overview about the robotic system. The integration to automatic recycling line, programing and manufacturing, are given in Sect. 4, and finally the conclusions are presented in Sect. 5.

2   Detection and Image Processing

The step of detecting the SUW begins with the capture of the image with a simple camera; then, images are preprocessed for neural network training and later they can be run in detection mode. Figure 1 conceptually shows the detection and image processing process. The complete procedure is in an infinite loop while the system is in operation. First, the image is captured from a camera with standard CMOS sensor [6]. In the second stage of the process and because the images are processed on a conveyor industrial whose background color is black, a way to facilitate processing of the images is to convert them to grayscale and have the background color perfectly identified. The next step is to equalize the image from its histogram [7] to reduce in acquisition process of the image, the different conditions to lighting that make the same image appears as a different image. The following two steps involve applying basic filters to eliminate noise and to smooth the contours of the image. The filtering stage is based in OpenCV library [8]. The penultimate stage is an algorithm to facilitate the training of the neural network, and facilitate recognition of SUW, in this step; the image

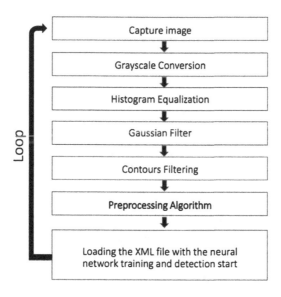

Fig. 1. Detection image process.

preprocessing is performed to continue the training of the neural network. The preprocessing algorithm is explained below.

2.1   Preprocessing Algorithm

After the image is captured, an image database is generated with the samples to preprocess. Figure 2 shows the flowchart of preprocessing algorithm. The image is binarized for quick processing. It begins to loop through the array of the image to find a pixel corresponding to an object; if the pixel is found, a counter is incremented and compared to a threshold in order to eliminate image noise or pixels that do not correspond to any real object; when the counter is greater than the threshold, a marker is inserted. The marker is a diagonal which size is chosen properly and should be greater than the threshold. The loop repeats until the image matrix is completed.

In Fig. 3 we can see the image through the preprocessing process. In subfigure (a) we can see an input image without any processing, below it, we see step five the diagram in Fig. 1, filtering contour. It can be easily seen in the bottom right, an apparent object corresponding to noise caused by lighting conditions. On the right side, we have the result with the preprocessing algorithm. Note that the spurious object disappears because the markers are placed only when there is a defined pixel threshold. The goal is to generate images similar to a rectangle.

2.2   Neural Network Training

For training the neural network, 60,000 samples images object were used to identify (positive images) and 30,000 images of the background color band and

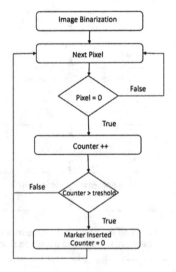

Fig. 2. Preprocessing algorithm flowchart.

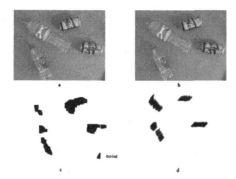

Fig. 3. Preprocessing image. Left side: no preprocessing algorithm; right side: output with preprocessing.

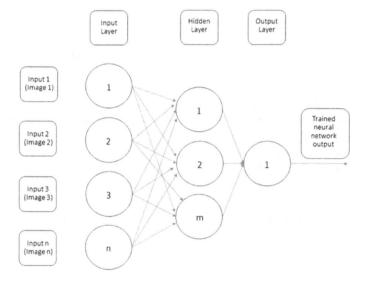

Fig. 4. Training the neural network

solid waste without the object to be identified (negative images). The support for the training of the neural network was by the Viola-Jones algorithm for face detection [9,10] and implemented on openCV. We use Haar-based cascade classifiers and store the trained classifier in XML file to later be used as classifier; last stage of identification and classification process as was shown in Fig. 1. The algorithm is basically a learning algorithm that uses the positive and negative images to train a classifier that can later be used to detect the objects in real time. Some binary rectangles are assigned to each image to create a unique identifier of the object. This is the main reason of preprocessing algorithm, to create images with semi-definite and rectangular images; the classifier becomes faster and more efficient. The network training is performed between the input layer and the hidden layer images, and according to information obtained from the positive images and negative images; you can generate a good classifier (Fig. 4). The neural network is trained specifically for detecting a single object. Table 1 shows the required values and used for to train the classifier on the OpenCV library.

Table 1. Critical train-cascade values.

Stages	Stage Type	Feature Type	HitRate	AlarmRate	WeightTrimRate
20	BOOST	HAAR	0,999	0,5	0,95

3   Robotic System

The general concept to automatic and robotic system is shown in Fig. 5; the proposal includes four Delta robots ABB and four cameras to SUW detection, a camera for each robot and for each material to be identified. The robotic system is capable of receiving the slot number that the band is divided, as we only have 10 possible positions, this is very easy to quantize and communicate. The ABB robot Delta controller is responsible for processing and it estimates the time of arrival at its operating range to gripper the objet. Each module Delta ABB has its own controller and follows the general sequence diagram described in Fig. 6. First, boot parameters are initialized, once initialized correctly, they check the communication link and control network; and manually or automatic mode is ready to receive the information of the identification system and run de conveyor tracking function.

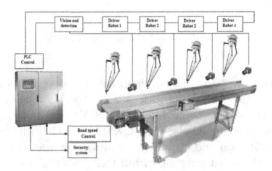

Fig. 5. General concept of recycling line.

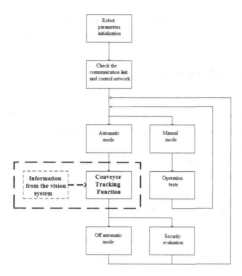

Fig. 6. Program sequence diagram.

4   Results

The automatic and robotic recycling line with vision system integrated (Fig. 7). Is composed of a conveyor belt of SUW, four robotic modules to grip objects and four identification systems. All this, integrated and automated for four types of solids recycled. The recycling line includes four containers where the delta robots

Fig. 7. (a) Automatic recycling line prototype. (b) Suction pad, for materials such as glass, paper or paperboard, and (c) gripper, for materials such as aluminum cans and plastic bottles.

deposit the selected materials; correct operation of the line is to receive SUW jumbled and separate in the containers autonomously.

4.1   Vision System Operation

The first tests of the system consisted in very contrasting objects with the background color. We show in Fig. 8, the identification and detection of one to multiple objects, alone and mixed with other objects. The software is able to identify up to 10 objects simultaneously.

After the first tests, the system was tested in the band with SUW. The final test can be seen in Fig. 9, where the correct identification of a waste aluminum is achieved, It can be seen the viewing area corresponding to $1\,m^2$ (right side of figure) and the imaginary slots, corresponding to the x coordinate. In the image, the robot only received the position: *slot3*.

4.2   Tracking Algorithm

To avoid sending y coordinate to robotic system, we thought of a simple tracking system. The identification system is capable of delivering the pair of

Fig. 8. First tests, detection of an object and multiple objects in laboratory. (a) a single objet, (b) multiple objects, and (c) multiple objects with noise.

Fig. 9. Test of identification.

coordinates (x, y). However, to only send a variable, in this case the x coordinate; we divide the camera vision area into slots; these slots are numbered from slot 1 to slot 10. Thus sending a single variable to the robotic system, the number of slot that corresponds to having only 10 points in the x-axis. This can be seen in Fig. 9. The position is detected immediately when the object enters in the vision area. The robotic system estimates the time between entering the object to the vision area until it can be gripped by the mechanism. With these simple steps, we save processing time, by the side of the system of recognition, and communication time between both systems, by the number of variables that will be sent.

Fig. 10. Robotic recycling line in operation with the vision and identification system.

4.3 Automatic and Robotic Recycling Line Operation

Finally, we tested the integrated system to verify accurate operation of the plant. Figure 10, show the identification system and delta robot gripper the selected object. The gripper transports a cardboard box, while the vision system identifies recycled aluminum. In this case the delay between the detection and the subjection is $2s$. The robotic system controller is adaptive to this delayed and can to grip more than one object in its operation area, depending on the band speed. In this case to $2\,km/hr$.

5 Conclusion

We developed, manufactured and implemented a line of separation of solid waste, using a vision system and identification of objects with delta robots that can process materials to recycle. We present the final satisfactory results. In a future work, we wish incorporate hyperspectral cameras to detect polymer families.

Acknowledgment. The authors wish to acknowledge the support of the CONACYT, within the program of incentives for innovation, ID: 222304 "recycling of municipal solid waste, with automated control and monitoring systems" and CIATEQ A.C. Aguascalientes.

References

1. Black, M.J., Yacoob, Y.: Tracking and recognizing rigid and non-rigid facial motions using local parametric models of image motion. In: Proceedings of the Fifth International Conference on Computer Vision, pp. 374–381, 20–23 June 1995
2. Ahmad, M., Lee, S.-W.: Recognizing human actions based on silhouette energy image and global motion description. In: 8th IEEE International Conference on Automatic Face & Gesture Recognition, FG 2008, pp. 1–6, 17–19 September 2008
3. Parikh, D.: Recognizing jumbled images: the role of local and global information in image classification. In: 2011 IEEE International Conference on Computer Vision (ICCV), pp. 519–526, 6–13 November 2011
4. Pulli, K., Baksheev, A., Kornyakov, K., Eruhimov, V.: Realtime computer vision with OpenCV. Commun. ACM **55**, 61–69 (2012)
5. Informe Residuos Solidos Urbanos, Estadístico. Secretaría de Medio Ambiente y Recursos Naturales SEMARNAT, México 2012 (2012). www.gob.mx/semarnat
6. Fossum, E.R.: CMOS image sensors: electronic camera-on-a-chip. IEEE Trans. Electron Devices **44**(10), 1689–1698 (1997)
7. Liangping, T., Dong, C.: Histogram equalization and image feature matching. In: 2013 6th International Congress on Image and Signal Processing (CISP), vol. 01, pp. 443–447, 16–18 December 2013
8. Bradski, G.: The OpenCV library. Dr. Dobb's J. Softw. Tools **25**(11), 120–126 (2000)
9. Viola, P., Jones, M.: Rapid object detection using a boosted cascade of simple features. In: Conference on Computer Vision and Pattern Recognition (CVPR), pp. 511–518 (2001)
10. Liao, S.C., Zhu, X.X., Lei, Z., Zhang, L., Li, S.Z.: Learning multi-scale block local binary patterns for face recognition. In: Lee, S.-W., Li, S.Z. (eds.) ICB 2007. LNCS, vol. 4642, pp. 828–837. Springer, Heidelberg (2007)
11. Lippmann, R.P.: An introduction to computing with neural nets. IEEE ASSP Mag. **4**(2), 4–22 (1987)

Face Recognition Using Histogram Oriented Gradients

Alberto Dzul Calvillo, Roberto A. Vazquez$^{(\boxtimes)}$, Jose Ambrosio, and Axel Waltier

Intelligent Systems Group, Facultad de Ingeniería, Universidad La Salle, Benjamin Franklin 47, 06140 Condesa, DF, Mexico
ravem@lasallistas.org.mx

Abstract. Face Recognition Systems has been applied in a wide range of applications. However, their efficiency drastically diminish when they are applied under uncontrolled environments such as illumination change conditions, face position and expressions changes. Because of that, it is necessary to evaluate the performance of different feature extraction techniques robust to this kind of transformations for its further integration to a Face Recognition System. In this paper, we study and evaluate the pertinence of using the Histogram Oriented Gradients (HOG) method as a feature extraction technique to deal with the transformations already mentioned. To measure the performance of the proposed feature extraction method, several experiments were performed using two databases: one database under a controlled environment taken from the literature and other built in our laboratory under a semi controlled environment. The experimental results show that using HOG combined with different distances classifiers provides better results than those achieved with the well-know Eigenfaces technique.

1 Introduction

In the last years, face recognition has been applied in several applications such as access control, video surveillance, multimedia, etc. However, there are still some challenges to be solved when these applications are used under uncontrolled environments such as illumination changes and face expression changes. These challenges demand the necessity of exploring new methods to describe a face in terms of features robust to changes in expressions and illumination. Face recognition methods for describing a face can be divided into two categories: holistic and feature-based. Perhaps, among the most popular holistic methods we could mention the well know eigenfaces technique and its variants [6,12] . In general, this type of techniques, project input faces onto a dimensional reduced space to build a feature vector to represent a face where recognition is performed. Although these technique provides a good performance under controlled environments, it is know that under uncontrolled environment its accuracy diminish due to they assume that a face is a static object that can be reconstructed with linear combinations of eigenfaces. On the other hand, feature-based approaches

© Springer International Publishing Switzerland 2016
A. Martin-Gonzalez and V. Uc-Cetina (Eds.): ISICS 2016, CCIS 597, pp. 125–133, 2016.
DOI: 10.1007/978-3-319-30447-2_11

use geometric relations among the facial objects such as eyes, lips, mouth, etc. to recognize a face. There are some works that uses geometric characteristic for the Face Recognition [14–16]. Other approaches use templates which are compared against a matrix that represents the face [11,17–19]. Although several works focus their effort in the feature extraction to outperform the face recognition systems [13,20,21] and some other work are focused in the classification algorithms such as Support Vector Machine (SVM), Radial Basis Function (RBF), and Artificial Neural Networks (ANN) [22–24], their application under uncontrolled environment is still a challenge. Descriptors based on Histogram of Oriented Gradient (HOG), which are invariant to illumination and rotation, has been applied in object recognition and pedestrian recognition [1,25–27]. Recently, HOG descriptors have been applied to face recognition. In [2] and [5], the authors also apply a regular grid to compute the HOG descriptors and study the effect of overlapping and angle orientation. In [3], the authors proposed an extension of HOG based on the co-occurrence matrix. In [4], the authors reduce the feature vector computed over a regular grid using fuzzy logic techniques and LDA, respectively.

This paper is focused on the robustness of the HOG descriptor as a feature extraction technique to deal with face recognition problems under illumination and expression changes. In contrast to previous related papers, nor normalization stage such as eyes alignment or common pixel resolution neither dimensional reduction is applied. At the same time, it is evaluated the rate of recognition when the windows size of the grid is changed. To measure the performance of the proposed feature extraction method, several experiments were performed using two databases: one database under a controlled environment taken from the literature and other built in our laboratory under a semi controlled environment. The content of this paper is organized as follow: in Sect. 2, the HOG descriptor is presented. In Sect. 3, we explained the proposed methodology to detect and recognize a face under a partially controlled environment. Section 4 presents the experimental setup and the discussion of the results. Finally, Sect. 5 presents the conclusions and ongoing research.

2   HOG Descriptor

The HOG descriptor is a local statistic of the orientations of the image gradients which is invariant to rotation and illumination changes. According to [28], the main idea behind this descriptor is that local object appearance and shape can often be characterized rather well by the distribution of local intensity gradients or edge directions. The HOG feature summarizes the distribution of measurements within the image regions and is particularly useful for recognition of textured objects with deformable shapes.

Basically, the HOG descriptor divides the image into many cells where a histogram counts the occurrences of pixels orientations given by their gradients. Finally, the HOG descriptor is built with combination of these histograms. Based on this process, four major steps can be delighted: image derivative computing, magnitude and gradient orientation computing, partial histograms building, and normalization of partial histograms.

For computing the derivative in the horizontal and vertical directions denoted with G_x and G_y, a Sobel filter over the input image I is performed.

After dividing the image into N cells, the next step of HOG feature is to compute the magnitude $|\nabla I(x,y)|$ and the orientation $\theta(x,y)$ of the gradient. The magnitude is given by:

$$|\nabla I(x,y)| = \sqrt{G_x^2 + G_y^2} \tag{1}$$

while gradient is given by:

$$\theta(x,y) = arctan\left(\frac{G_x}{G_y}\right) \tag{2}$$

After that, the gradient angles in each cell are quantized into a number of bins B of regularly spaced orientations and the magnitudes for identical orientations are accumulated into a histogram. For each pixel with coordinates (x,y) it is determined which of the B orientations is the closest to its orientation $\theta(x,y)$ and then its magnitude $|\nabla I(x,y)|$ is added to the corresponding bin. The number of bins B used indicates the length of the histogram vector for each cell.

For better invariance to illumination and noise, a normalization step is usually used after calculating the histogram vectors. A common normalization scheme is computed as:

$$V_n = \frac{V}{\sqrt{\|V\|^2 + \epsilon^2}} \tag{3}$$

where V is the vector to be normalized and ϵ is a small positive value needed when evaluating empty gradients.

Briefly, we could follow the next steps to perform the calculation of HOG descriptor:

1: Compute the derivative in the horizontal and vertical directions
2: Compute the magnitude and the orientation of the gradient
3: Quantize into bins orientation
4: Normalize descriptor

Each pixel has to vote for some orientation in the histogram channels, this could be done based on the orientation of the gradient and the votes are added for the channels and for the cells. The cells could be radial o rectangular. The orientations could be separated between 0 and 180° or 0 and 360°, depending on the use of the sign. Interpolation could be done over neighbors. The vote is a function of the magnitude of the gradient of the pixel, could be the magnitude itself, the square of the magnitude or the magnitude squared.

3   Pattern Classification

Pattern classification is useful to determine to which class belongs a given pattern. Basically, the method is to collect the data, then extract the representative pattern information and then decide the class that it belongs to. Classes are a set of patterns that share characteristics and differentiate between them. There are different methods to decide the class to which a pattern belongs; one of them is to calculate the distance between the given pattern and the classes reference patterns. Two of the most popular distance metrics are presented in Eqs. 4 and 5.

The Euclidean distance allows finding how different is a pattern from another considering them as vectors. In the case of pattern classification, the pattern where the minimal distance to the reference class vector was computed, is the class to which the pattern belongs.

$$d\left(p, q\right) = \sqrt{\left(p_1 - q_1\right)^2 + \ldots + \left(p_n - q_n\right)^2} \ . \tag{4}$$

The Mahalanobis distance is also used to find the minimal distance between two patterns but it takes into account the correlation between the database. The Mahalanobis distances of an observation x from a set of observations with mean μ and a covariance matrix S is defined as shown in Eq. 5:

$$D_M\left(x\right) = \sqrt{\left(x - \mu\right)^T S^{-1} \left(x - \mu\right)} \ . \tag{5}$$

4   Methodology

Due to the face recognition system captures a picture that contains not only the face but several other objects, first, it is necessary to localize the face. For this purpose the Viola-Jones algorithm was used [9]. Then an image preprocessing technique could be applied to the image. In our case, we do not apply any preprocessing technique with the purpose of evaluating how much robust is the HOG feature extraction technique under partially controlled environments. The next step is to compute a feature vector using the HOG feature extraction technique over the region that contains the detected face. Once all the features of each face have been obtained, the next step is to perform the classification stage. This stage is composed of two phases, the training phase and the testing phase. During the training phase, the average feature vector for each class is computed whereas during the testing phase, the distance among an unknown face and the average vector of each class is computed.

Figure 1 described the steps of the proposed methodology.

Fig. 1. Proposed methodology

5   Experimental Results

To evaluate the accuracy of the proposed methodology, several experiments using two different datasets were performed. To validate statistically the behavior of the proposed methodology, 30 experiments using the same configuration were done. On each of these experiments, we randomly generate two different sets of data, 50 % of the patterns for training set and the remaining 50 % for the testing set.

One of the datasets used during the experiments was taken from the AT&T lab and contains a set of images snapped between April 1992 and April 1994 [7]. This dataset is composed of 40 classes, with 10 samples of each class. The main characteristics of this dataset are that it was built using a homogenous background, the pictures were snapped in different times, different positions of the face are presented, and variations in illumination, but not many; the expressions in the face are different, and some people use fixtures like glasses. Also there are men and women. The age of the subjects varies and some people have beard and/or mustache. The resolution of the images is the same for all samples and it is 92×112 with 256 gray levels. Some images of this database are shown in Fig. 2.

To evaluate the proposed methodology under a partially controlled environment, the ULSA dataset was created in our labs. For this dataset more complex features were added. The background of the images is not homogeneous, lighting conditions are adverse, the expressions are also more marked than AT&T dataset, the camera distance is different between each snapshot, the resolution of the image changes, and some are not too good focused. This database is composed of 10 classes with 20 samples per class. Some images of this dataset are shown in Fig. 3.

Fig. 2. Samples of ORL data base

Fig. 3. Samples of ULSA data base

Fig. 4. Examples of the construction of the cells

In order to understand how much affect the number of windows during the HOG descriptors calculation process, we varied the number of windows on the height and width. For that purpose, three different experiments were done, dividing the face region into 5×5 windows, 10×10 windows and finally, 15×15 windows, see Fig. 4. The histograms were normalized but no overlap between cells so that only contribute to a block. The histogram is divided into nine channels between 0 and 180°, so that the magnitude of angle is considered unsigned. After computing the HOG descriptor, we generate a vector of 225, 900 and 2025 features for 9 channels when the face region was divided into 5×5, 10×10 and 15×15 windows, respectively.

Once obtained the feature vector, we compute an average vector from all patterns that belong to a given class using the training dataset. Then, the euclidean distance between each pattern from the testing dataset and the means of all classes is computed to get the class of the pattern. For the case of Mahalanobis distance, we compute the mean as well as the covariance matrix using the training dataset. It is important to mention that instead of computing the inverse of the covariance matrix, the pseudo-inverse is calculated for this work. After that, the distance of each of the patterns of the test dataset is computed to determines the class.

In Table 1, the average recognition results obtained using HOG and distances are presented.

Table 1. Average results using HOG

Dataset	Euclidean		Mahalanobis	
	Tr. cr	Te. cr	Tr. cr	Te. cr
ATT(5×5)	0.9877	0.9093	1.00	0.8463
ULSA(5×5)	0.7911	0.6633	1.00	0.8830
ATT(10×10)	0.9858	0.8701	1.00	0.9772
ULSA(10×10)	0.9030	0.7579	1.00	0.9307
ATT(15×15)	0.9890	0.8474	1.00	0.9748
ULSA(15×15)	0.9159	0.7741	1.00	0.9357

Tr. cr = Training, Te. cr. = Generalization.

In order to compare the results, we applied the well-known principal component analysis (PCA) [6, 8, 10]. Several experiments using PCA were done with the purpose of presenting a comparison against other feature extraction methods and show the robustness of HOG descriptor under partially controlled environment. Table 2 presents the results obtained using PCA.

Table 2. Results using Eigenfaces

Dataset	Euclidean		Mahalanobis	
	Tr. cr	Te. cr	Tr. cr	Te. cr
ATT(80 %)	0.9785	0.8951	0.8506	0.6950
ULSA(80 %)	0.8650	0.7306	0.51.26	0.4453
ATT(90 %)	0.9873	0.8971	0.82.00	0.6556
ULSA(90 %)	0.8953	0.7543	0.49.06	0.4100
ATT(100 %)	0.9926	0.9040	0.78.45	0.6043
ULSA(100 %)	0.9113	0.7583	0.46.33	0.3866

Tr. cr = Training, Te. cr. = Generalization.

As it was shown in Tables 1 and 2, using the reference dataset, the method with the highest percentage is HOG using the Mahalanobis distance in the training stage where 100 % was obtained. For the testing phase remains HOG being better with 97.72 %. For the dataset build in our lab, in both training and testing HOG was better, with a maximum in tests of 93.57 % correct classification, while with the use of PCA percentage fell to 75.83 % Comparing the percentages obtained using Mahalanobis, we can observe that the use of a larger number of windows increases the recognition rate.

As can be seen from the results obtained with the proposed methodology, HOG descriptors provides better results compared against those obtained using PCA.

6   Conclusions

Based on the experimenta results, we observed that the gradients orientation histogram technique is useful for the face recognition problem. This paper verifies in an experimental framework that HOG can be used to efficiently classify distinct classes of the same object, particularly in the context of face recognition. This technique is efficient, considering that the achieved recognition rates were above 90 % with both distances. HOG descriptor tends to be more stable than PCA, which could not successfully classify the dataset in a partially controlled environment. On the other side, when a face is well placed inside the image, HOG can be used since it obtains the faces orientations and is robust amongst different conditions of the image.

Acknowledgment. The authors would like to thank CONACYT-INEGI and Universidad La Salle for the economical support under grant number 187637, I-061/12 and NEC-03/15, respectively.

References

1. Dalal, N., Triggs, B.: Histograms of oriented gradients for human detection. In: Computer Vision and Pattern Recognition, CVPR 2005, vol. 1, pp. 886–893 (2005)
2. Salhi, A.I., Kardouchi, M., Belacel, N.: Fast and efficient face recognition system using random forest and histograms of oriented gradients. In: BIOSIG 2012, pp. 1–11 (2012)
3. Thanh-Toan, D., Kijak, E.: Face recognition using co-occurrence histograms of oriented gradients. In: ICASSP 2012, pp. 1301–1304 (2012)
4. Salhi, A.I., Kardouchi, M., Belacel, N.: Histograms of fuzzy oriented gradients for face recognition. In: ICCAT 2013, pp. 1–5 (2013)
5. Shu, C., Ding, X., Fang, C.: Histogram of the oriented gradient for face recognition. Tsinghua Sci. Technol. **16**(2), 216–224 (2011)
6. Yu Zhujie, Y.L.: Face recognition with eigenfaces. In: IEEE International Conference on Industrial Technology, pp. 434–438 (1994)
7. AT&T Laboratories Cambridge (1994). http://www.cl.cam.ac.uk/research/dtg/attarchive/facedatabase.html
8. Turk, M.A., Pentland, A.P.: Face recognition using eigenfaces. In: CVPR 1991, pp. 586–591 (1991)
9. Viola, P., Jones, M.: Robust real-time face detection. In: ICCV 2001, vol. 2, p. 747 (2001)
10. Abdi, H., Williams, L.J.: Principal Component Analysis (2010)
11. Torres, L.: Is there any hope for face recognition? (2000)
12. Bansal, A., Mehta, K., Arora, S.: Face recognition using PCA and LDA algorithm. In: ACCT 2012, pp. 251–254 (2012)
13. Quellec, G., Lamard, M., Cazuguel, G., Cochener, B., Roux, C.: Fast wavelet-based image characterization for highly adaptive image retrieval. IEEE Trans. Image Process. **21**(4), 1613–1623 (2012)
14. Yikui, Z., Junying, G., Junying, Z., Ying, X.: Disguised face recognition via local phase quantization plus geometry coverage. In: ICASSP 2013, pp. 2332–2336 (2013)
15. Badakhshannoory, H., Safayani, M., Manzuri-Shalmani, M.T.: Using geometry modeling to find pose invariant features in face recognition. In: ICIAS 2007, pp. 577–581 (2007)
16. Xiaoming, L., Tsuhan, C.: Pose-robust face recognition using geometry assisted probabilistic modeling. In: CVPR 2005, vol. 1, pp. 502–509 (2005)
17. Karungaru, S., Fukumi, M., Akamatsu, N.: Face recognition using genetic algorithm based template matching. In: ISCIT 2004, vol. 2, pp. 1252–1257 (2004)
18. Cook, J., McCool, C., Chandran, V., Sridharan, S.: Combined 2D/3D face recognition using log-gabor templates. In: AVSS 2006, p. 83 (2006)
19. Levada, A., Correa, D.C., Salvadeo, D.H.P., Saito, J.H., Mascarenhas, N.: Novel approaches for face recognition: template-matching using dynamic time warping and LSTM neural network supervised classification. In: IWSSIP 2008, pp. 241–244 (2008)
20. Yunfei, J., Ping, G.: Comparative studies of Feature Extraction methods with application to face recognition. In: IEEE International Conference on Systems, Man and Cybernetics, 2007, ISIC, pp. 3627–3632, 7–10 October 2007

21. Sheeba Rani, J., Devaraj, D., Sukanesh, R.: A novel feature extraction technique for face recognition. In: International Conference on Computational Intelligence and Multimedia Applications, 2007, vol. 2, pp. 428–435, 13–15 December 2007
22. Jondhale, K.C., Waghmare, L.M.: Improvement in PCA performance using FLD and RBF neural networks for face recognition. In: ICETET 2010, pp. 500–505 (2010)
23. Faruqe, M.O., Hasan, M.A.M.: Face recognition using PCA and SVM. In: ASID 2009, pp. 97–101 (2009)
24. Chengliang, W., Libin, L.,Yuwei, Z., Minjie, G.: Face recognition based on principle component analysis and support vector machine. In: ISA 2011, pp. 1–4 (2011)
25. Vimal, S.P., Ajay, B., Thiruvikiraman, P.K.: Context pruned histogram of oriented gradients for pedestrian detection. In: International Multi-Conference on Automation, Computing, Communication, Control and Compressed Sensing (iMac4s), 2013, pp. 718–722, 22–23 March 2013
26. Suard, F., Rakotomamonjy, A., Bensrhair, A., Broggi, A.: Pedestrian detection using infrared images and histograms of oriented gradients. In: Intelligent Vehicles Symposium, 2006 IEEE, pp. 206–212 (2006)
27. Haengseon, S., Seonyoung, L., Jongchan, C., Kyungwon, M.: Efficient pedestrian detection by Bin-interleaved histogram of oriented gradients. In: TENCON 2010, pp. 2322–2325 (2010)
28. Shu, C., Ding, X., Fang, C.: Histogram of the oriented gradient for face recognition. Tshinghua Sci. Technol. 16(2), 216–224 (2011)

An Approach to Codification Power on the Behavior of Genetic Algorithms

Y.El. Hamzaoui[1(✉)], J.A. Rodriguez[2], S.A. Puga[1],
M.A. Escalante Soberanis[3], and A. Bassam[3]

[1] Posgrado en Ciencias de la Ingeniería, Instituto Tecnológico de Tijuana, Tijuana, Mexico
youness@tectijuana.edu.mx, srgpuga@gmail.com
[2] Centro de Investigación en Ingeniaría y Ciencias Aplicadas,
Universidad Autónoma del Estado de Morelos, Cuernavaca, Morelos, Mexico
jarr@uaem.mx
[3] Facultad de Ingeniería, Universidad Autónoma de Yucatán, Mérida, Yucatán, Mexico
{mauricio.escalante,Baali}@correo.uady.mx

Abstract. Genetics Algorithms (GAs) are based on the principles of Darwins evolution which are applied to the minimization complex function successfully. Codification is a very important issue when GAs are designed to dealing with a combinatorial problem. An effective crossed binary method is developed. The GAs have the advantages of no special demand for initial values of decision variables, lower computer storage, and less CPU time for computation. Better results are obtained in comparison the results of traditional Genetic Algorithms. The effectiveness of GAs with crossed binary coding in minimizing the complex function is demonstrated.

Keywords: Genetic Algorithms · Crossed binary coding · Mathematical functions

1 Introduction

In mathematics, a function is a relation between a given set of elements called the domain and a set of elements called the codomain. The function associates each element in the domain with exactly one element in the codomain. The elements so related can be any kind of thing (words, objects, qualities) but are typically mathematical quantities, such as real numbers. The concept of function can be extended to an object that takes a combination of two (or more) argument values to a single result. This intuitive concept is formalized by a function whose domain is the Cartesian product of two or more sets. A linear function, whose graph is a straight line which has an equation that can be written in the form of: However, equations whose graphs are not straight line or they are called nonlinear functions, some non linear functions have specific names. For example, a quadratic function is non linear and it has an equation in the form of: where Another nonlinear function is a cubic function which has an equation in the form of:, where. In mathematics and computer science, optimization, or mathematical programming, refers to choosing the best element from some set of available alternatives. Combinatorial

© Springer International Publishing Switzerland 2016
A. Martin-Gonzalez and V. Uc-Cetina (Eds.): ISICS 2016, CCIS 597, pp. 134–142, 2016.
DOI: 10.1007/978-3-319-30447-2_12

optimization is a branch of optimization. Its domain is optimization problems where the set of feasible solutions is discrete or can be reduced to a discrete one, and the goal is to find the best possible solution. In the simplest case, this means solving problems in which one seeks to minimize or maximize a real function by systematically choosing the values of real or integer variables from within an allowed set.

This formulation, using a scalar, real-valued objective function which is probably the simplest example; the generalization of optimization theory and techniques to other formulations comprises a large area of applied mathematics. More generally, it means finding "best available" values of some objective function given a defined domain, including a variety of different types of objective functions and different types of domains.

The increasing importance of nonlinear programming with mathematical programming (MP) is commonly used [1]. Because of the nonlinearity nature in minimization the complex function, unbearable long computation time will be induced by the use of MP when the nonlinear function is somewhat complicated [2]. Severe initial values for the optimization variables are also necessary. Moreover, with the increasing size of the nonlinear function, MP will be futile. Heuristics needs less computational time, and severe initial values for optimization variables are not necessary, but it may end up with a local optimum due to its greedy nature. Also, it is not a general method with respect to the fact that special heuristic rules will be needed for a special problem [3]. Many authors applied traditional Genetics Algorithms (GAs) to solve the problem. Traditional GAs performs effectively and gives a solution within 0.5 % of the global optimum. However, traditional GAs has the disadvantage of long searching time and so needs more CPU time. The application of GAs analysis to solve complicated problems has been the subject of numerous review articles. The article published by Çelebi Mehmed describes the new approach based on two explicit rules of mendel experiments and mendel's population genetics for the genetic algorithm [4]. However, we have seen, to solve the proposed problem more effectively, we apply GAs with crossed binary coding method which is developed, an intelligent problem-solving method that has demonstrated its effectiveness in solving complicated problem, and satisfactory results are obtained.

The rest of this paper is organized as follows. Section 2 presents the methodology including the new codification to demonstrate the effectiveness of GAs with crossed binary coding in solving the proposed problem, Sect. 3 presents four problems with three objective functions and their computations results using GAs with crossed binary coding in comparison with traditional GAs are also given. Finally, the conclusions on this work are drawn.

2   Methodology

2.1   Genetics Algorithms

The term genetics algorithms, almost universally abbreviated now a days to GAs, was first used by John Holland and his colleagues [5]. A genetics algorithms is a search technique used in computing to find exact or approximate solutions to optimization and search problems, however the canonical steps of the GAs can be described as follows:

The problem to be addressed is defined and captured in an objective function that indicated the fitness of any potential solution.

A population of candidate solutions is initialized subject to certain constraints. Typically, each trial solution is coded as a vector X, termed a chromosome, with elements being described as solutions represented by binary strings. The desired degree of precision would indicate the appropriate length of the binary coding.

Each chromosome, Xi, $i = 1,...,$ P, in the population is decoded into a form an appropriate for evaluation and it is then assigned a fitness score, $\mu(Xi)$ according to the objective.

Selection in genetics algorithms is often accomplished via differential reproduction according to fitness. In a typical approach, each chromosome is assigned a probability of reproduction, Pi, $i = 1,...,$ P, so that its likelihood of being selected is proportional to its fitness relative to the other chromosomes in the population. If the fitness of each chromosome is a strictly positive number to be maximized, this is often accomplished using roulette wheel selection [6]. Successive trials are conducted in which a chromosome is selected, until all available positions are filled. Those chromosomes with above-average fitness will tend to generate more copies than those with below-average fitness.

According to the assigned probabilities of reproduction, Pi, $i = 1,...,$ P, a new population of chromosomes is generated by probabilistically selecting strings from the current population. The selected chromosomes generate "offspring" via the use of specific genetic operators, such as crossover and bit mutation. Crossover is applied to two chromosomes (parents) and creates two new chromosomes (offspring) by selecting a random position along the coding and splicing the section that appears before the selected position in the first string with the section that appears after the selected position in the second string and vice versa (see Fig. 1). Bit mutation simply offers the chance to flip each bit in the coding of a new solution.

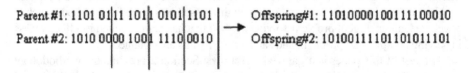

Fig. 1. Four-points crossover operators

The process is halted if a suitable solution has been found or if the available computing time has expired, otherwise, the process proceeds to step 3 where the new chromosomes are scored, and the cycle is repeated.

2.2 Implementation and Empirical Methods

Mapping Objective Functions to Fitness Form. In many problems, the objective is more naturally stated as the minimization of some cost function g(x) rather than the maximization of some utility or profit function u(x). Even if the problem is naturally stated in maximization form, this alone does not guarantee that the utility function will be non negative for all (x) as we require in fitness function (a fitness function must be a non negative figure of merit [5]. In normal operations research work, to transform a minimization problem to a maximization problem we simply multiply the cost function by a minus one.

In genetic algorithm work, this operation alone is insufficient because the measure thus obtained is not guaranteed to be non negative in all instances. With GAs, the following cost-to-fitness transformation is commonly used:

$$f(x) = C_{max} - g(x) \quad \textit{when } g(x) < C_{max}$$
$$= 0 \quad \textit{otherwise}$$

may be taken as the largest g value observed thus far. For the problem of nonlinear function in this paper, we take this transformation form.

Fitness Scaling. In order to achieve the best results of GAs, it is necessary to regulate the level of competition among members of the population. This is precisely what we do when we perform fitness scaling. Regulation of the number of copies is especially important in small population genetic algorithms. At the start of GAs runs, it is common to have a few extraordinary individuals in a population of mediocre colleagues. If left to the normal selection rule $(pselecti, = f_i/\sum f)$, the extraordinary individuals would take over a significant proportion of the finite population in a single generation, and this is undesirable, a leading cause of premature convergence. Later on during a run, we have a very different problem. Late in a run, there may still be significant diversity within the population; however, the population average fitness may be close to the population best fitness. If this situation is left alone, average members and best members get nearly the same number of copies in future generations, and the survival of the fittest necessary for improvement becomes a random walk among the mediocre. In both cases, at the beginning of the run and as the run matures, fitness scaling can help.

Constraints. We deal with the dimension constraints by coding equations and deal with time constraints this way: a genetics algorithm generates a sequence of parameters to be tested using the system model, objective function, and the constraints. We simply run the model, evaluate the objective function, and check to see if any constraints are violated. If not, the parameter set is assigned the fitness value corresponding to the objective function evaluation. If constraints are violated, the solution is infeasible and thus has no fitness.

Codings. When GAs manages a practical problem, the parameters of the problem are always coded into bit strings. In fact, coding designs for a special problem is the key to using GAs effectively. There are two basic principles for designing a GAs coding [6]: (1) The user should select a coding so that short, low order schemata are relevant to the underlying problem and relatively unrelated to schemata over other fixed positions. (2) The user should select the smallest alphabet that permits a natural expression of the problem. Based on the characteristic and structure of nonlinear function, instead of choosing the concatenated, multiparamerted, mapped, fixed-point coding, crossed binary coding is designed according to the two principles above. The coding method of a nonlinear function is as follows: The studied case considers two optimization variables encoded using a binary system, which consists in altering one bit of each variable. Then we place the highest bit of reach local string at the site from 1st to nth in nonlinear function chromosome and place the second highest bit of each local string at the site from $(n + 1)th$ to $2nth$, and so on. Then we can obtain a nonlinear function chromosome (see Fig. 2).

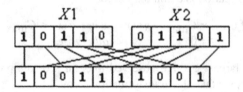

Fig. 2. Illustration of the encoding method for a small size example

The reason for using crossed binary coding, because this codification is suitable for the continuous and discontinuous variables, and can be analyzed in theory as follows:

- Because of the strong relationship among the parameters, the highest bit in each local string in binary codings determines the basic structure among every parameter, and the second highest bit in each local string determines finer structure among every parameter, and so on for the third, the forth, etc.
- The schema defining length under crossed coding (n) is shorter than the length under concatenated, mapped, fixed-point coding $(nK-K + 1)$.

According to the schema theorem: short schemata cannot be disturbed with high frequency, the schema under crossed coding has a greater chance to be reproduced in the next generation. Due to its combining the characteristics of function optimization with schema theorem and successful binary alphabet table, crossed coding demonstrates greater effectiveness than the ordinary coding method in our implementation.

Local string formation is achieved this way: for a parameter $x \in [x_{min}, x_{max}]$ that needs to be coded, transform it to a binary coding $X \in [0, 2^K]$ first (appropriate length K is determined by the desired degree of precision) and then map it to the specified interval $[x_{min}, x_{max}]$. In this way, the precision of this mapped coding may be calculated as $\delta = (x_{max} - x_{min}/2^K - 1)$.

In fact, this means that the interval from x_{min} to x_{max} is divided into $2^K - 1$ parts, because the biggest binary string that has a length of K equals the decimal number $2^0 + 2^1 + 2^2 + \ldots + 2^{K-1}$. Then, we can obtain $x = x_{min} + \delta X$, and a local string for parameter x with a length of K is obtained.

To illustrate the coding scheme to the size variables more clearly, we also want to give a simple example. For the minimization problem: min $z = f(x, y)$ in which $x \in [300, 700]$ and $y \in [700, 1200]$, if we adopt a string length of 5 for each local string and X:10110, Y:01101 is an initial solution, we will get the chromosome 1001110001 (see Fig. 3) and obtain:

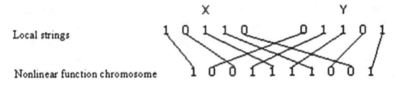

X   Y

Local strings

Nonlinear function chromosome

Fig. 3. Multiparameter crossed binary codings

$x = x_{min} + \delta_x X = 300 + \left[(700 - 300)/(2^5 - 1)\right] (2^4 \times 1 + 2^3 \times 0 + 2^2 \times 1 + 2^1 \times 1 + 2^0 \times 0)$

$\quad = 300 + (400/31) \times 22$

$\quad = 583.871$

$y = y_{min} + \delta_y Y = 700 + \left[(1200 - 700)/(2^5 - 1)\right] (2^4 \times 0 + 2^3 \times 1 + 2^2 \times 1 + 2^1 \times 0 + 2^0 \times 1)$

$\quad = 700 + (500/31) \times 13$

$\quad = 909.677$

Reproduction. The reproduction operator may be implemented in algorithmic form in a number of ways. In this paper, we take the easiest methods Roulette wheel [6].

Crossover. Crossover operator can take various forms, i.e., one-point crossover, multi-point crossover [7]. It is commonly believed that multi-point crossover has better performance. The number of crossover points in a multi-points crossover operator is determined by the string structure. In this paper, four-points crossover operator is adopted. The crossover rate plays a key role in GAs implementation. Different values for crossover rate ranging from 0.4 to 1.0 were tried, and the results demonstrate that the values ranging from 0.6 to 0.95. In this paper, we take 0.6 as a crossover rate.

Mutation Operation. After selection and crossover, mutation is then applied on the resulting population, with a fixed mutation rate. The number of individuals on which the mutation procedure is carried out is equal to the integer part of the value of the population size multiplied by the mutation rate. These individuals are chosen randomly among the population and then the procedure is applied.The mutation rate using in this paper is 0.40.

Elitism. The elitism consists in keeping the best individual from the current population to the next one. In this paper, we take 1 as elitism value.

2.3   Population-Related Factors

Population Size. The GAs performance is influenced heavily by population size. Various values ranging from 20 to 200 population size were tested. Small populations run the risk of seriously under covering the solution space, a small population size causes the GAs to quickly converge on a local minimum, because it insufficiently samples the parameter space, while large populations incur severe computational penalties. According to our experience, a population size range from 50 to 3000 is enough our problem. In this paper and according to our experience, we take 200 as a population size.

Initial Population. It is demonstrated that a high-quality initial value obtained from another heuristic technique can help GAs find better solutions rather more quickly than it can from a random start. However, there is possible disadvantage in that the chance of premature convergence may be increased. In this paper, the initial population is simply chosen by random.

Termination Criteria. It should be pointed out that there are no general termination criteria for GAs. Several heuristic criteria are employed in GAs, i.e., computing time (number of generations), no improvement for search process, or comparing the fitness of the best-so-far solution with average fitness of all the solutions. All types of termination criteria above were tried; the criteria of computing time are proven to be simple and efficient in our problem. In our experience, 200–10000 generations simulation is enough for a complicated problem as our problem. The best results were obtained when the numbers of generations were taken as 10000 for our problem. However, we need to stress that the Genetics Algorithms parameters for traditional GAs and GAs with crossed binary coding are the same. As shown in Table 1 presents the Genetic Algorithms parameters used in this study.

Table 1. Genetic algorithms parameters

Population size	3000
Generation number	10000
Survival rate	0.15
Mutation rate	0.001
Elitism	1

3   Examples and Analysis

Four problems are given here to demonstrate the effectiveness of GAs. The mathematical functions are composed of four problems with three objective functions, each one depending on two independent variables $(X_1$ and $X_2)$, the choice of these mathematical functions is due to their particular behavior [8]. The results are presented in Table 2.

From these results, we can see that better results are obtained in comparison with the traditional Genetic Algorithms. In addition, GAs with crossed binary coding results in a faster convergence and the computing time is less than that of traditional GAs. This demonstrates the effectiveness of GAs with crossed binary coding in solving the complicated problem quickly.

Now, several works about some important aspects in our implication of GAs and some problems in practice. The most important of all is the method of coding. Because of the characteristics and inner structure of the nonlineal function, the commonly adopted concatenated, multiparamerted, mapped, fixed point coding is not effective in searching for the global optimum as soon as possible. However, as is evident from the results of application, crossed binary coding method is well fit for the proposed problem.

Table 2. Results founded by traditional GAs and GAs with crossed binary coding

Functions	Variable X1	Variable X2	Minimum	CPU time(s)* GAs(a)	GAs(b)
Problem 1					
$f_1 = \dfrac{(x_1-2)^2}{2} + \dfrac{(x_2+1)^2}{13} + 3$	2	-1	3	10	<1
$f_2 = \dfrac{(x_1+x_2-3)^2}{36} + \dfrac{(-x_1+x_2+2)^2}{8} - 17$	2.5	0.5	17	13	<1
$f_3 = \dfrac{(3x_1-2x_2-1)^2}{175} + \dfrac{(-x_1+2x_2)^2}{17} - 13$	0.5	0.25	-13	17	<1
$x=(x_1,x_2)\in[-4,4]^2$					
Problem 2					
$f_1 = \dfrac{(x_1-2)^2}{2} + \dfrac{(x_2+1)^2}{13} + 3$	2	-1	3	10	<1
$f_2 = \dfrac{(x_1+x_2-3)^2}{36} + \dfrac{(-x_1+x_2+2)^2}{8} - 17$	2.5	0.5	-17	13	<1
$f_3 = \dfrac{(3x_1-2x_2+4)^2}{18} + \dfrac{(x_1-x_2+1)^2}{27} + 15$	-2	-1	15	20	<1
$x=(x_1,x_2)\in[-4,4]^2$					
Problem 3					
$f_1 = \dfrac{x_1^2}{2} + \dfrac{(x_2+1)^2}{13} + 3$	0	-1	3	10	<1
$f_2 = \dfrac{x_1^2}{2} + \dfrac{(2x_2+2)^2}{15} + 1$	0	-1	1	10	<1
$f_3 = \dfrac{(x_1+2x_2-1)^2}{175} + \dfrac{(2x_2-x_1)^2}{27} - 13$	0.5	0.25	-13	15	<1
$x=(x_1,x_2)\in[-4,4]^2$					
Problem 4					
$f_1 = 0.5(x_1^2+x_2^2)+\sin(x_1^2+x_2^2)$	0	0	0	10	<1
$f_2 = \dfrac{(3x_1-2x_2+4)^2}{8} + \dfrac{(x_1-x_2+1)^2}{27} + 15$	-2	-1	15	20	<1
$f_3 = \dfrac{1}{(x_1^2+x_2^2+1)} - 1.1\exp(-x_1^2-x_2^2)$	0	0	-0.1	25	<1
$x=(x_1,x_2)\in[-4,4]^2$					

*CPU time was calculated to this method on Microsoft Windows XP Profesional Intel(R)D CPU 2.80 Ghz, 2.99 GB of RAM.GAs(a): Traditional GAsGAs(b): GAs with crossed binary coding.

Another aspect that affects the effectiveness of genetic procedure considerably is crossover. Corresponding to the proposed coding method, we adopted a four point crossover method. It is commonly believed that multi-point crossover is more effective than the traditional one point crossover method. Nevertheless, we find that it is not the case that the more points to crossover, the better. It is also important to note that the selection of crossover points as well as the way to carry out the crossover should take in account the bit string structure, as is the case in our implication. Despite the demonstrated advantages of GAs algorithms, the feeling persists that there is much to learn about effectively implementing a genetic algorithms. One problem in practice is the premature loss of diversity in the population, which results in premature convergence. Because premature convergence is so often the case in the implementation of GAs according to our computation experience. Something has to be done to prevent it. Our experience makes it clear that the elitism parameter could solve the premature problem effectively and conveniently.

4   Conclusions

Genetics Algorithms are applied to minimize nonlineal function. Satisfactory results are obtained. The obtained experimental results showed that the performance of the GA depends on the codification chosen. Moreover, crossed binary coding method is the best schema, with this codification GAs converges faster and the computing time is less than that of traditional GAs. However as it does not seem easy to envisage a method to select in advance the best schema for a given problem instance, in principle the only way is trying various schemas at the same time and take the value provided for the best one. The only answer that we can give to this problem is based on Darwin's principle of natural selection. The idea is that in any population of self-reproducing organisms, there will be variations in the genetic material and upbringing that different individuals have. These differences will mean that some individuals are better able than others to draw the right conclusions about the world around them and to act accordingly. These individuals will be more likely to survive and reproduce and so their pattern of behavior and thought will come to dominate.

References

1. Wang, C., Quan, H., Xu, X.: Optimal design of multiproduct batch chemical process using genetic algorithm. Ind. Eng. Chem. Res. **35**(10), 3560–3566 (1996)
2. El Hamzaoui, Y., Hernandez, J.A., Cruz-Chavez, M.A., Bassam, A. Search for Optimal Design of Multiproduct Batch Plants under Uncertain Demand using Gaussian Process Modeling Solved by Heuristics Methods. Chem. Prod. Process Model. 5(1) (2010)
3. Patel, A.N., Mah, R.S.H., Karimi, I.A.: Preliminary design of multiproduct non-continuous plants using simulating annealing. Comput. Chem. Eng. **15**, 451 (1991)
4. Çelebi, M.: A new approach for the genetic algorithm. J. Stat. Comput. Simul. **79**(3), 275–297 (2009)
5. Holland, J.H.: Adaptation in Natural and Artificial Systems. University of Michigan Press Inc., Ann Arbor (1975)
6. Goldberg, D.E.: Genetic Algorithms in Search Optimization and Machine Learning. Addison Wesley Publishing Company Inc., Chicago (1989)
7. Frantz, D.R.: Non-Linearities in Genetic Adaptive Search. Academic Press Inc., San Diego (1994)
8. Viennet, R.: Nouvel outil de planification experimentale pour l'optimisation multicritere des procedes. These de doctorat, INP Lorraine, France (1997)

Author Index

Printed in the United States
By Bookmasters